FIRST to the FLAMES

The History of Fire Chief Vehicles

Edward L. Peterson

Published by

**krause
publications**

700 E. State Street • Iola, WI 54990-0001
Telephone: 715/445-2214

Please, call or write us for our free catalog of antiques and collectibles publications. To place an
order or receive our free catalog, call 800-258-0929. For editorial comment and further information,
use our regular business telephone at (715) 445-2214

Library of Congress Catalog Number: 99-61453
ISBN: 0-87341-674-0

Printed in the United States of America

CONTENTS

DEDICATION

Dedicated to my grandchildren: Lee, Joshua, Scott,
Alan, Benjamin, Kenneth, Ryan, Edward, Bethany,
and the memory of Lee E. Peterson

Lee at 18 months.

ABOUT THE AUTHOR

The author is currently a self-employed training consultant for several major local industries, while serving as Senior Vice-President and Archives Chairman for SPAAMFAA (Society for the Preservation and Appreciation of Antique Motor Fire Apparatus in America). This organization has over 3,200 members worldwide. He writes the "Archives" column for the Society's publication, *Enjine-Enjine*.

At the age of 16, he began as a volunteer fireman and earned a training certificate from the Pennsylvania State Fire School. This sparked a lifetime interest and everlasting love of fire apparatus and mechanisms, which led to the antique automobile hobby. The author graduated from a vocational school, and enjoyed the machine trade. He served in the U.S. Army and began a career in aircraft operation and maintenance. He retired from the Army in 1984 as Chief of the Aircraft Shops Division, at New Cumberland Army Depot, New Cumberland, Pennsylvania.

In 1986, the author was chairman of the Antique Automobile Club of America's fall meet in Hershey, Pennsylvania. He was antique car registration chairman for nine years, and was elected to the executive board of AACA Hershey Region for twelve years, and is a past president.

In 1975, the author bought his first antique vehicle from the Washington Fire Company #8 in Lebanon, Pennsylvania. It was a 1948 American LaFrance Model 775 pumper, and he still maintains and drives it. He also has his first car, a 1949 Dodge business coupe, which was destined to be a fire chief car, along with several other antique cars.

Shortly after the delivery of the 1948 pumper, the author joined the Pennsylvania Pump Primers and became active in the muster circuit. He is currently President of the Pennsylvania Pump Primers, which is the Central Pennsylvania Chapter of SPAAMFAA.

Besides his interest in building and design, the author is also an avid collector of Winross model trucks, and fire toys.

He is married to Tookie and has three sons and nine grandchildren.

After taking thousands of photographs of fire apparatus and antique automobiles, it was the author's dream to combine the two into the subject of this book.

The author's 1948 American LaFrance pumper, from Lebanon, Pennsylvania, alongside the Ford Bronco that serves the Chief of Lebanon Bureau of Fire.

Edward L. Peterson

COVER STORY

Philadelphia's Deputy Fire Commissioner George E. Hink stands beside his 1952 Buick Roadmaster, posed in front of the fountain at Logan Circle in 1952. He later became Fire Commissioner, April 24, 1964.

George Edward Hink was born May 15, 1898, and lived his whole life in the Kensington section of Philadelphia. He started his fireman career in the Philadelphia Fire Department at the age of 23. He was promoted to Lieutenant six years later, and advanced to Captain in 1931 while assigned to Engine 13. Hink was 42 when he was named Battalion Chief. He was appointed Acting Deputy Chief at the age of 44, and held that post until 1947. In March of 1952, he was named Chief of the Department by Mayor Clark. Chief Hink died May 23, 1965.

Chief Hink was a "fireman's fireman" as reported in the March 1965 issue of *Flame.* Many stories have been told of his sixth sense for danger and his ability to always remain cool and collected at the fire scene. He became a legend in his own time.

His greatest achievement after becoming Fire Chief in 1952 was rebuilding a strong department under his leadership. He told the *P.F.D. News*, "It was one of the proudest moments of my life, when I was named Deputy Commissioner in charge of fire fighting. Here was my chance to help make this department the best in the country." He played a strong role in the new scheme of things with a new City Charter and a new City Administration. New equipment and apparatus were ordered and put in service. Supplies and working materials were put on a monthly delivery basis. A station building and rehabilitation program was started. In 1960, he had 267 pieces of apparatus and 2,894 men under his command. As the years rolled on, the improvements soon turned the department into one of the best rated in the world.

Chief Hink came up through the ranks to the highest position in the department and could understand the problems and the true feelings of the men and women who served under him. He had the administrative ability to tackle the problems of logistics and personnel and still lost none of the enthusiasm for fire fighting. He was truly a "fireman's fireman!"

Chief Hink and his wife, Mary, had three children and eleven grandchildren. His son, George Victor, followed in his father's footsteps with a career in the fire department. Thanks go to Michael Hink for sharing his memories of his grandfather.

Chief Hink can be seen in action on the "Firefighting in Philadelphia, Waterfront Fires 1959-1971" videotape, produced by The Ahrens-Fox Video Library.

The 1952 Buick Roadmaster Chief's car on the front cover was photographed equipped with a Roto-ray light in the middle between a large locomotive bell with an American eagle top, and a Federal "Q" siren. The car is equipped with a full-width upper bumper bar and a Mars DX-40 unit on the roof. This car was powered by an inline eight-cylinder engine with Dynaflow drive. The building in the background is the Free Library of Philadelphia.

The modern yellow minivan is a 1998 Ford Windstar assigned to the fire marshal at Logan International in Boston, Massachusetts. Minivans have become popular with their convertible seating and cargo space.

The black-and-white photograph is a Reo Model T-6 from Rome, New York. The Chief and his driver are waiting patiently, with the top down during a snowstorm, for this picture to be taken. Note the chains on all four wheels. This was a common safety practice during this era.

BACK COVER

The top black-and-white photo is a White assigned to the Chief Engineer of the Philadelphia, Pennsylvania Fire Department.

The other black-and-white photo shows the 1948 Chrysler sedan used by Fire Chief Earl Swartz of Harrisburg, Pennsylvania.

The color photo shows a 1957 Pontiac Super Chief station wagon assigned to the Training Division of the Hartford, Connecticut Fire Department. It previously served the Deputy Chief. A Federal Model 17 Roto-Light is mounted on the roof. The apparatus in the background is a B Model Mack Pumper.

ACKNOWLEDGMENTS

I would like to extend my sincere appreciation to all those who made this massive undertaking a reality. It would have been impossible to gather and assemble the extensive collection of photographs and material needed, without the help of friends and fellow fire buffs. I must thank the photographers from the beginning to the end of this century, who aimed their cameras at "Buggies," "Wagons," and especially, the Chief's "Automobiles."

Those of you who preserved the images of time must share with the early photographers, who, in absentia, recorded history for all of us to enjoy and treasure.

Special thanks go to Scott Schmipf for our new-found friendship and for his huge collection of photos, as well as the precision models that he allowed me to photograph. Without his contribution, this book would have lacked the quality and attention it deserves. To an indispensable friend, Kim Miller of the AACA Library & Research Center, who assisted in the research and encouraged me with articles and history on automobiles. To Jeanne Smith, associate editor of *Antique Automobile*, for her guidance. To Michael Hink, whose grandfather graces the front cover with his 1952 Buick. Not only did he supply the photograph, but also the life history material of a fire fighter who rose to the highest rank of "Chief."

To my valued friends in the Pennsylvania Pump Primers, James Derstine, David Buskey, David Houseal, and Harvey Eckart, who provided support and ideas along with photos and material. Their dedicated years of fire fighting and their profound interest in preserving the heritage of our fire service greatly contributed to the making of this book.

I want to thank the many members of the Society for the Preservation and Appreciation of Antique Motor Fire Apparatus in America who answered the alarm in the "Archives" column of *Enjine-Enjine*, especially Marvin Cohen, Mae and Dan Martin, Matt Lee, Editor Walt McCall, Glenn Banz, Frank Tremel, Paul Romano, Bill Cary, Roger Birchfield, Edward Frey, Bob Schierle, John Schmidt, Charles Black, Steve Cloutier, William Schwartz, William Killen, Randy Wootton, John Dorgan, Tim Elder, Tommy Herman, Robert Potter, William Wilcox, Craig Stewart, Richard Story, Charles Seaboyer, W.G. Garrison, Bill Egan, Mark Boock, Don Abrahamson, Ray Pitts, Richard Adelman, John A. Calderone, Roger Bjorge, Jackson Gerhart, Howard Brenner, Bare Cove Museum, Aston McKenney, Daniel Jasina, Eric Hansen, Don Jarvis, Wayne Kidd, Parker Browne, Wayne Sorensen, David Schell, Harry Rosenblum, The Racine Firebell Museum, Bill Noonan, Alex Matches, B.A. Harper, Louis Nelson, Toledo Firefighters Museum, Jack Ramsey, Charles W. Reynolds, Ronald Jeffers, Bob Muller, Dale Magee, Ed Haas and the late Jim Burner.

Among the others who deserve special credit for their excellent photography are Steve Loftin, John D. Floyd, Jr., Arthur Knobloch, the late Glen Alton, Dick Bartlett, Ron Bogardus, Ernest Rodriques, Hank Sajovic, John M. Calderone Robert M. Washburn and my father, Kenneth Peterson.

Many thanks also go to the individuals and associations who opened their highly prized collections to be included in the pages of this book, namely Herb Brawley and the Long Beach Museum, T.J. Carpenter, Gene Conway, Ed Effron, Bill Elliott, Paul Fox, Fred Fuston, Greater Harrisburg Fire Museum, John J. Robrecht, Keith Marvin, Gordon J. Nord, Jr., Shelton Hensley Family, Christian Ulvog of the ISO office, Ralph Harkins, Karl Krouch, R.D. Jennings, Hank Knight, Robert Kulp, Jack Lerch and the George Mand Library & Research Center of FDNY, Jack Paxton, William Phillips, J.F. Repp, John J. Schaler III, Bill Snyder, Charles H. Fewster, Ken Little, James T. Coyne, York Fire Museum, Robert Washburn, Box 388 Productions, Thomas Engle, Walt Schryver, Michael Rybarczyk, Ron Helman, Leo Duliba, the late Len Sasher, Edward Christopher, Wayne Stuart, Deran Watt, Bob Willever, and William Witt.

My sincere gratitude to a high school buddy and longtime friend, Dick Mann, who came to my aid using his keyboard, and also my daughter-in-law, Cathy, who professionally used her typing skills to compile the research material.

And last but not least, my heartfelt thanks and hugs to my wife, Tookie, who continued to have patience with me over the four years it took to assemble this project.

I apologize to any contributor whose name is not listed.

The Chief, Bob Camp, and his driver, Frank Yockers at a 1915 fire scene in Salina, Kansas. Photo courtesy Tom Girard

INTRODUCTION

The idea for this book came from my association with the Antique Automobile Club of America (AACA) and the Society for the Preservation and Appreciation of Antique Motor Fire Apparatus in America (SPAAMFAA).

It was my dream to combine the two hobbies into a book under one cover. The AACA's automobile research library was only a short distance from my home, and the opportunity presented itself to collect the material for this book. At the time, no books were available on fire chief cars among the vast number of titles of fire-related books.

Shortly after I started the search for Chief car photos, I discovered that the photographers of the past favored fire trucks and apparatus, not the Chief cars. The search for good photos would take longer to assemble than originally planned. Although members of SPAAMFAA answered the alarm sounded in the fire publications for photos, it took several years to acquire the photographs in this book.

My goal was to fill the pages of this book with as many different makes as possible. The end result provides ten decades full of photographic history, plus a restored section, with an introduction to each period. It is interesting to see how the departments became motorized and how the hometown loyalty to car manufacturers occurred. As the decades evolve, it is equally interesting to see the design changes and advancements of the Chief cars in the 20th century. The variety of bells, sirens, and lights is amazing, while the markings and lettering are as varied as the colors in which they are painted.

Information presented with the photographs received was checked for accuracy. Often, the cars or persons in the photos were not identified, and endless hours of research ensued to ensure the information printed would be accurate.

The restored Chief car section provides a look at the parade and muster cars that have been rebuilt to emulate the "Chief's Buggy." It is an exciting part of the antique automobile hobby.

The section on toys, scale models, and pedal cars is included to augment interest in "Fire Chief" cars. It explores the variety of collectibles in different sizes and materials, but by no means covers the spectrum of collectibles available in today's market.

The last section of this book provides Chief car information taken from national reports on hundreds of city fire departments. This reference material was compiled beginning in 1904 and is both educational and fascinating, as well as a bit humorous.

Edward L. Peterson

Author holding one of the framed Chief car pictures sent to him for use in this book.

HISTORY LOG

The 20th century changed the horse- and hand-drawn fire apparatus into a modern fire fighting machine with capabilities far exceeding the engineering of 1900. The horses used for pulling the apparatus to the fire and back were part of the daily life of the fireman, and each horse had a name and stall to rest. The horse chosen to pull the Chief's buggy was a favorite, gentle around children, and stood hitched and ready to serve every day. The Chief sometimes used his personal horse and buggy, but most of the major city departments had assigned horses and buggies for the Chief officers.

Then it happened!

A well-to-do person in the town bought a machine that used gasoline purchased from the drugstore, and drove it past the fire station on his way to church. The noise attracted everyone's attention and the smell was different. The horseless carriage age had arrived, and it didn't take long for the Chief of the Department to get his "Buggy."

Becoming a Motorist

City fire departments assigned drivers, who studied manuals and took lessons from the car manufacturer, before driving the Chief.

Instructions for the Operation of Overland Cars

Rules of the Road

Before venturing upon the highway, an important thing for the novice is to acquaint himself with the various and universally observed rules of the road. Motorists are law-abiding as a class and none but the reckless will refuse or neglect to pay obedience to the rules established by law or custom for the guidance of all users of roads.

When meeting another vehicle, coming from the opposite direction, it is the rule of the road in the United States for both vehicles to **keep to the right**, each turning to one side of the center of the road, as shown in Fig. 30.

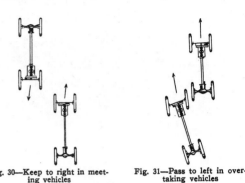

Fig. 30—Keep to right in meeting vehicles

Fig. 31—Pass to left in overtaking vehicles

If the other vehicle be a horse-drawn vehicle, heavily laden or incapable of turning out for some reason or other, common courtesy will prompt the automobilist to permit that vehicle to keep the center of the road and pass it by going clear over to the right, even though this should involve traveling on the poorer portion of the highway.

In overtaking slower-going vehicles traveling in the same direction, it is the rule to **pass to the left**. (Fig. 31.)

It is likewise a mere courtesy, and in some localities even a law, that one traveler shall not hold the road to the exclusion of other travelers, but shall **turn whenever possible**, to permit the vehicle following him to pass. It is a fact that more accidents are caused by vehicles crossing in front of others than in any other manner.

(Taken from 1913 operations manual.)

Deputy Chief McDonough with his driver, Boston, Massachusetts. Photo courtesy Bill Noonan

In smaller fire companies, the Chief drove the automobile himself. Sometimes he was elected the town fire chief because he owned a motor car and could drive it. He was able to travel further, carry small fire extinguishers, and get to the fire faster. *The Colonist* of December 1909 quoted Chief Thomas Davis as saying, "My idea would be to have a two-seat machine of a runabout pattern. I could reach a fire in the shortest possible time and hold it in check until the arrival of other apparatus." (Henry Ford built the Model T Chemical Wagon on this premise.)

The automobile proved itself early in the fire departments, yet horses would be needed to pull the large and heavy apparatus such as the steam pumpers until the automotive engineers built larger and stronger tractor- and truck-type equipment. Teams of horses were still used in great numbers as late as 1915. It was hard for the fireman to see "Joe" and "Charlie" sold at a public auction. Many of the horses never forgot the fire bell sound, and it was common to see the horses galloping to a fire with their new owner's wagon in tow.

"Joe," like a good sport, tries to shake hands with his victor, who ousts him from his job at No. 11 Engine Company.

Car Assignments

The large city fire departments had a staff of Chief Officers who required transportation on a daily basis. To cite an example: Atlanta, Georgia, had a fire force of 124 men and 48 horses in 1905. The Chief had three Asst. Chiefs. The records show only one Chief's Wagon in service and one in reserve. Both were kept at fire headquarters. Asst. Chiefs rode on the apparatus stationed in their quarters. By 1954, the Chief and Asst. Chief on duty were each provided with a 1950 Oldsmobile sedan and the Battalion Chiefs on duty had a 1951 Buick and 1951 Oldsmobile. A 1952 Chevrolet sedan was provided for the arson investigator and a 1937 LaSalle was assigned to the Superintendent of Repairs. A 1948 Oldsmobile sedan was used as a spare Chief's car. (Excerpts from the Underwriters Reports.) So as the cities' fire departments grew, so did the number of automobiles employed.

Normally the higher priced and newer car would be assigned to the chief, and his older car would be placed in reserve or handed down to other, lower ranking officers.

Captain   **Ass't Chief**   **Chief**

The rank of officers in the fire department depends on roster setup and number of divisions and level of supervision. Each rank has a different insignia and the uniforms may be different.

The more buttons on the chief officer's coat, the higher the rank, and the more trumpets on the insignia, the higher the rank. Later, the dress uniform jacket sleeves would have the rank in stripes. Earlier, small hash marks on the sleeves would indicate years of service.

The fire department chain of command was respected as in any military-type department, and the directives at the fire scene and in the offices flowed down to the fire fighter. The morale and discipline of the department is maintained through this structure.

As history unfolds photographically within these pages, the cars assigned to many different levels of chief officers are depicted. The Chief Engineer was an early title given to the head of the department, because it related to the college level of engineering study needed to understand and operate the apparatus, in addition to the administrative duties of the office. Chief of the Department, Deputy Chief, Assistant Chief, and Battalion Chief cars are shown throughout the book. The Superintendent of Repairs and the Fire Alarm Superintendent and Fire Marshal also would be provided automobiles in larger city departments.

Four Cylinder, 45 Horse-power Roadster

CHIEF'S CAR

EVER since there have been fire departments, the first man to answer a call has been the Chief. The minute an alarm is turned in, it is the duty of the officer in charge to rush to the scene of action, at top speed. He should be on the ground and have his plan of action in mind, if possible, before the rest of the department arrives. The saving of time means money, and often, lives, in fighting a conflagration, and it is up to the chief to see that not a second is wasted in directing his attack.

The modern conveyance for the chief is the automobile roadster. It must be speedy, easy to operate and absolutely dependable. The White roadster meets these requirements and has the added advantages of economy and long service.

In large cities, the chief, or one of his assistants, is required to make the rounds of the various stations each day, in addition to answering all calls. For this use, which requires hard, uninterrupted service, the White roadster is exceptionally fitted.

White roadsters are being used in many cities throughout the country and in every case they have given unqualified satisfaction.

These chief's cars may be had with two or four passenger bodies and with 30, 45 or 60 horse-power motors. They can also, if desired, be equipped with a chemical tank, reel or basket, hose, etc., hand extinguishers, or other small equipment.

White company advertisement courtesy Paul Romano

Purchasing

What makes an automobile a Chief's car? A few fire apparatus manufacturers did produce a small quantity of Chief cars. Both Seagrave and Ahrens Fox Chief cars are included in this book. Neither was successful in marketing this type vehicle and dropped the idea. The bulk of the automobiles sold to fire departments came from local dealers, and the passing of the keys from the dealer salesperson to the Chief would make it official.

In the early years, many towns and cities had a number of car manufacturers within the city limits. Fire departments were most times loyal to a carmaker in their city, and even carried advertisement on the car for the company. It's been reported that some fire departments were given Chief cars, on the condition that the manufacturer could use it for publicity.

An example of a local manufacturer was Cole Motor Car Co., (1909-1925). The Indianapolis Fire Department used Cole and Stutz automobiles, both manufactured in Indianapolis, Indiana.

Cole roadsters without lighting. Photo courtesy Leroy Cole

Cole stock certificate.

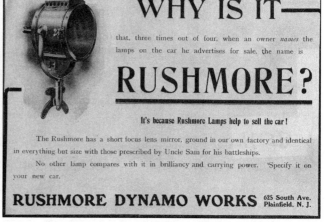

Rushmore Dynamo Works lamp for Cole automobile.

The 1930's depression changed the local brand loyalty forever. The number of car manufacturers declined due to mergers and bankruptcies. Fire departments purchased the cars offered through established dealers. Sometimes the cars came to the fire department from the police department, after the police received new cars. The radios were installed, and what better way to economize the city budget than give the fire department the police specials.

Group purchasing through the state governments for standard full-size sedans and 4x4 vehicles is the latest budget tool for purchasing. Finally, the 1990s has a different approach to new Chief and Incident Command cars. Several private companies are customizing new SUVs for fire department command cars, and they bulk purchase certain models. These companies modify the SUVs with control consoles, custom cabinetry, and install emergency lightbars, warning lights and paint or apply computer-cut decals for outside markings.

Service and Care

Put yourself in the shoes of a Chief of a large city fire department in the year 1911. You recently purchased a new car, which was quoted to have a top speed of 40 miles per hour. This top speed was the reason for selecting this particular make of automobile. During the acceptance trial, your driver raced the car to its top speed and it never reached the required stated speed. What do you do? The Chief of the District Fire Department of Washington wrote a letter directly to the president of the Carter Motor Car Corp. A copy of the return letter, signed by President A. Gary Carter, is proof that the "Chief" can get results, and it's okay to go right to the top!

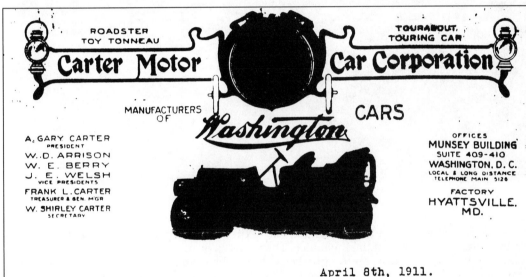

ROADSTER
TOY TONNEAU

TOURABOUT,
TOURING CAR

Carter Motor **Car Corporation**

MANUFACTURERS OF

Washington

CARS

A. GARY CARTER
PRESIDENT
W. D. ARRISON
W. E. BERRY
J. E. WELSH
VICE PRESIDENTS
FRANK L. CARTER
TREASURER & GEN. MGR
W. SHIRLEY CARTER
SECRETARY

OFFICES
MUNSEY BUILDING
SUITE 409-410
WASHINGTON, D. C.
LOCAL & LONG DISTANCE
TELEPHONE MAIN 5128

FACTORY
HYATTSVILLE,
MD.

April 8th, 1911.

Chief Frank J. Wagner,

District Fire Department,

Washington, D. C.,

Mr Dear Mr. Wagner:

Your letter of April 5th received, and contents noted. We are surprised to learn that your car is not now making the desired speed. Will state that this must be because same requires some adjustments, and we will be only too glad to remedy same at any time it is convenient to you.

Very respectfully,
Carter Motor Car Corporation

President.

Dictated.A.G.C.-M.

**Letter courtesy
Frank Tremel**

During the lifetime of any car many things could occur to it. Some things are unavoidable, such as damage from floods or a tornado. The Chief's car could have the same type of damage, but when the Chief and his car arrive at the fire scene, anything can happen! The accompanying photo of a Battalion Chief and remaining shell of his car tells a grim story. The Chief is surveying the remains of his sedan, which is burnt out from the top down. The attachment he had for his car is evident by the way he is surveying the damage. The bell and the maltese cross plate of the New York Fire Department along with the front bumper, reflects a ghost-like image lingering in the still water.

Maintenance

Vehicle maintenance is also an important item during the life of the Chief car. The first generation of motorized equipment required simple, but frequent, maintenance. The term "fix or repair daily" was a common factor on the early automobiles. Records were kept on the number of times the automobile wouldn't start when the alarm sounded. It was important that the Chief's car would start and get out of the station before the horses. Tinkering and tightening was routine with these machines. As the mechanical engineering improved on cars, less time was spent on daily items, and more attention was paid to engine and driveline maintenance.

**Photo courtesy
John M. Calderone**

Large city departments have repair crews and large machine shops to keep the "in service" vehicles operational. The city of New York has its own tow trucks to bring disabled Chief cars and fire apparatus back to the repair facility. The accompanying photo shows the 22nd Battalion Chief's Suburban being retrieved.

Small towns hired the local garage mechanics to perform repairs and install equipment.

The local new car dealers share a strong bond with their customers, and if the fire department is a new car customer, the service department normally responds quickly when needed. They feel the same urgency to be up and running for the next alarm. With the electronic controls and complex electrical systems on today's vehicles, the dealer service department and the fire department repair shops can find the trouble promptly using on-board diagnostic systems. Chief cars have become complex machines, but at the same time, car maintenance has progressed to a higher level. 1999 vehicles have the first engine tuneup interval at 100,000 miles, with routine fluid and filter changes.

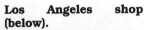

New York shops and Los Angeles shops both have separate areas for car maintenance. The FDNY stock room lower left has a large inventory of brake discs.

Los Angeles shop (below).

The repair shops not only perform maintenance, but also install equipment and accessories on the new deliveries. The car arrives clean, but without the attachments that are necessary to fulfill the Chief's needs: A siren: hand cranked, motor driven, or electronic. Warning lights: flashing, oscillating, or rotating. The emergency lightbar or strobes. Transferable equipment and radios for communications. Add to the list, any painting or lettering, decals, stripes, reflective material for night safety and any insignias or logos. Sometimes other unusual accessories are installed for comfort and safety, as the accompanying photos show.

The Muffler Cut-Out

Ordinarily the gases exhausted by the engine are passed into the atmosphere through a muffler, sometimes also misnamed the "silencer." The cut-out is a simple valve, which, when opened, permits the exhaust gases to escape without passing through the muffler.

Since even the best-designed of mufflers cannot perform its work without a certain back-pressure against the engine pistons, an unmuffled exhaust results in a slight increase of power, which may become of value in climbing hills. Also, the fact that an unmuffled exhaust is noisy is utilized when an attempt is made to see whether a cylinder is misfiring. Besides this, the cut-out muffler serves as a signal of warning on the road.

While the muffler cut-out has its advantages, its indiscriminate use, as in going through a community at night, etc., is apt to make it a nuisance to others within ear-shot. However, for purposes of testing the ignition and in touring through open country it is very useful.

The muffler cut-out of the Overland is actuated by a lever protruding through the floor board. Pushing the lever **forward** opens the valve. The lever may be kept in place by pushing it into a notch in the slot. To close the valve again, release the lever with a movement of your foot from **Fig. 29** right to left, as shown in Fig. 29.

Custom cabinetry to outfit interior space for command mission.

An early invention applied to the exhaust system to bypass the muffler. It did a good job of serving as a signal for the chief cars.

A winter apron installed to shield the passengers from the cold winter air. Photo courtesy Bill Noonan

Disposal

In the end, not many Fire Chief cars are restored. The fire departments in the early years of the century had few automobiles as reserves, so when the new car arrived, the old one was put to use performing duties as a "shop runner," or mechanic's rig. As an example, this book includes different photos of the same 1930s Packard from Albany, New York, with both "Chief" and "Repair Shop" lettering on the door. The emergency warning siren and light is shown in both photos.

Many large-frame Chief cars, such as 1930s Packards, Lincolns, and Studebakers were modified after their use as the Chief's car was over. They were fitted with truck bodies and other paraphernalia by the department shops. They served the fire alarm electrician, or just general shop hauling. After World War II, the cars were sold at public auctions. These cars were passed down through several public offices before they reached their demise at the auction lot. The cars most times were purchased by salvage buyers. The holes left in them by removing the bells and sirens discouraged many private buyers.

When a small department needs to sell the Chief's car, and it has low mileage and was well maintained, it usually is sold through a bidding procedure. This method ensures receiving the highest possible amount from those persons who bid. Advertisements placed in fire-related publications solicit a sealed bid to be opened in view of the officers, and they decide if the highest bid is accepted or rejected.

Amber folding arm light assembly, on FDNY Battalion Chief's Suburban.

The public envisions the Chief's car only as a means of speedy transportation to the fire or emergency scene. This is only one of many duties for the Chief's "Wagon." The administrative duties surrounding the office requires visits to other city and town fire departments to create mutual aid agreements, and survey business sites. Periodic and sometimes daily inspection trips are necessary to ensure fire prevention measures are being observed. The Chief is expected to periodically visit all fire stations and training sites. The Deputy or Battalion Chief may be delegated to perform some of these duties, so their cars are on the street serving the city's neighborhoods. The accompanying panoramic photo was taken at the FDNY Fire Academy located on Randalls Island, New York. These Chief vehicles brought together the officers of many fire departments from the surrounding areas for a day seminar at the fire academy.

We are about to enter the 21st century, holding the memories from the past 100 years shown on the pages of this book. The motorization and advancement in the past century has taken us from horse-drawn buggies to powerful, self-starting cars that we can drive sitting in luxurious comfort. It is unknown what the future will bring to this automotive segment of public service. In any event, the change will reflect the needs of the growing prevention and protection services of our fire departments and their "Chief cars."

EARLY YEARS OF MOTORIZATION: 1900-1910

At the turn of the century, most city and volunteer fire departments were totally dependent on the well-trained horses. The Chief was no exception with many uses for his horse drawn "buggy." Sometimes the Chief's buggy was his own personal carriage, but in most city departments, the buggy was bought and maintained by the city. This era of horse drawn buggies would continue well into the Teens for many of the departments.

The first motorized apparatus began to appear in the larger cities as chemical wagons on automobile-type chassis, and these same automobiles with seating became the "Chief's Buggy." As this era unfolded, many horse drawn buggies were kept in reserve, as records were compiled on the new machines to justify the reliability of this new technology. It didn't take long for the motorized Chief to enjoy the benefits of the automobile. Many new makes were built during this period, but only a few names, such as Buick, Cadillac, and Ford, would survive the century. The Chief and/or a driver aide are proudly posed for most of the photographs in this section.

This picture is typical of fire department equipment and uniform officers and men at the turn of the century. The Chief's single hitch buggy stands beside the triple hitch steamer and hose wagon in front of Engine Co. 3 firehouse in Washington, D.C. A foot-operated gong is mounted on the front panel of the four wheel buggy. Photo courtesy Library of Congress collection

Chief Tom Lane of the Manchester, New Hampshire Fire Department with his heavy-duty rubber tired buggy. A kerosene lantern is mounted on the rear of the seat. The white stallion appears to be well groomed and healthy. Photo courtesy Paul Romano collection

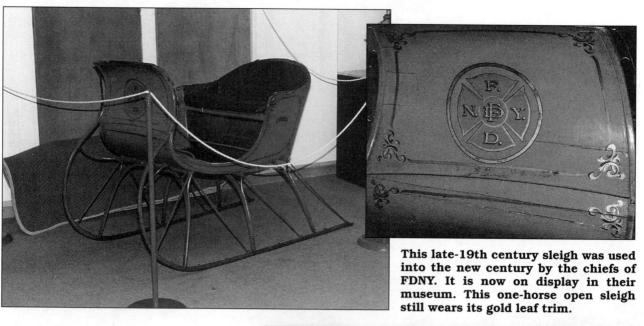

This late-19th century sleigh was used into the new century by the chiefs of FDNY. It is now on display in their museum. This one-horse open sleigh still wears its gold leaf trim.

Harrisburg, Pennsylvania Fire Department Chief John C. Kindler posed for this 1911 photograph in his rubber tired buggy. A foot-operated gong helps clear the way. Carriage lamps graced both sides of the seat, but proved dim defense against awaiting perils after sundown. The gong and lamps were later moved to the first motorized Chief's car, a 1913 Studebaker. Photo courtesy David Houseal collection

This Scranton, Pennsylvania Chief's buggy was purchased in 1907 from the G.F. & R.G. Stewart Co., Syracuse, New York. It was still in service when this photograph was taken of Asst. Chief Peter J. Roasar, Driver Charles Schneider and the gray mare in 1914 in front of fire headquarters. Note the leather fenders on the rear wheels, the Fire King lantern and a polished brass gong. The buggy is also equipped with a manual speed control (whip). Photo courtesy Mark Boock

FDNY Fire Chief Croker is steering his own private 1902 Locomobile Steamer with Captain Oswald as his passenger. This famous photograph records the first automobile used in the fire department. It was reported on December 31, 1899, that he passed the civil service exam with a 98+ score to become New York City's first fire chief in the new century. Photo courtesy the George F. Mand Library and Research Center of New York

Horse and carriage prepared for Chief Belt's funeral parade. His horse is covered with a black laced blanket and has polished black hooves. The aide, wearing his driving gloves, will walk the empty carriage to the Chief's last resting place. The Chief's parade hat and white high eagle helmet are positioned on the empty seat. The city of Washington D.C. would take delivery of its first motorized automobile for the Chief Engineer during this period of time. Photo courtesy Jackson H. Gerhart collection

Another early motorized four wheeler was this De Dion-Bouton Tandem Quadcycle used by the Boston, Massachusetts Fire Department Superintendent of Repairs. It was first produced in 1897. Photo courtesy Bill Noonan

THE FIRST MOTORIZED FIRE APPRATUS IN THE UNITED STATES

Fire Chief Walter Randlett is at the tiller of this 1903 Model C Stanley Steamer. It was the first motorized vehicle for the Newton, Massachusetts Fire Department, complete with mounted fire extinguisher. It is no surprise the department selected a Stanley, since they were built in Newton. Three hundred "C" models with a two-cylinder 6-1/2-horsepower engine were built. Photo courtesy New England Fire & History Museum Collection

Chief Charles Swingley of St. Louis, Missouri Fire Department with his driver in a 1905 Model "E" Locomobile. This 20-horsepower black touring car cost $2,000 new. It was placed in reserve in 1907 and sold in 1912. Photo Courtesy P.T. Nauman

When FDNY purchased this American Mercedes in 1905, it was considered a sport/luxury automobile. It was built by the Daimler Manufacturing Co., located in Long Island City, to the exact specifications of the German Mercedes. Mercedes red was the standard color for this $7,500 automobile. Note the Sterling Model 12 siren mounted in front of the gas headlamps, and the locomotive-type bell mount attached to the dashboard. Photo courtesy the Mand Library and Research Center of New York

Boston also purchased several Ross Steamers in 1906 built in nearby Newtonville, Massachusetts. This touring car weighed 2,800 pounds and cost one dollar per pound. (L-R) Fire Commissioner Ben Wells, "Bob" (the dog), Chief of the Department John Mullen, Driver Joe Webber, and Mr. Ross, owner of the automobile company. A large bell is mounted in front on the frame. Note the small BF monogram on the side door. Photo courtesy Bill Noonan

Photo taken years later of the same vehicle. Large script letters, side mounted lamps, spare tire, chains and Fire King lantern added. Photo courtesy Bill Noonan

This 1906 Baker Electric roadster was built in Cleveland, Ohio, for the Boston, Massachusetts Fire Department. Baker was famous for racing. It was steered by a tiller, but had a driveshaft and differential for the powertrain. Photo courtesy Boston FD Archives

FDNY purchased many different makes of automobiles in the early years. This c.1906-08 Berliet Double Phaeton waits outside the Brooklyn Fire Headquarters. This car was built by the American Locomotive Auto Co. of Providence, Rhode Island. Photo courtesy the Mand Library & Research Center of New York

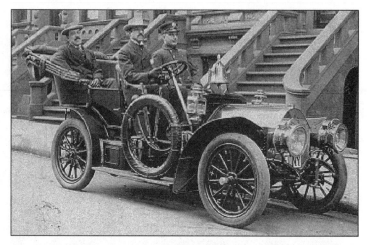

The Nation's Capital Fire Department purchased a two-engine Carter Car for the Chief Engineer, which was made during 1907-08 in Hyattsville, Maryland. This eight-cylinder 60-horsepower vehicle could run on one or both engines, using the same theory as dual ignition, to boost reliability and sales. Photo courtesy Len Sasher collection

Although a FDNY plate and locomotive bell are attached to this c.1907 Locomobile, it was reported to be owned by the famed Dr. Harry Archer. This Model "E" touring car cost $2,800 with a four-cylinder 20-horsepower engine. Photo courtesy of the Mand Library & Research Center of New York

This steam-powered 1907 White carries Deputy Chief Engineer August Emrich on his duties in the City of Baltimore, Maryland. The large bell is securely braced to the radiator shell. Deputy Chief lettering is painted on the side of the front seat bucket. Photo courtesy Bill Snyder

New York also purchased this 1907 Oldsmobile from the Olds Motor Works, Lansing, Michigan, for its fire department officers. This Model A Flying Roadster weighed 2,200 pounds and cost $2,750. The mounted bell was supplemented by an early electric siren. Photo courtesy the Mand Library & Research Center of New York

St. Louis 1907 Locomobile on parade. Photo courtesy P.T. Nauman

"Easily the best built car in America" was the slogan of this 1907 Locomobile used by the St. Louis Fire Department Chief. Shown at the scene of a fire, it continued in "A" service until 1912. After three years of reserve duty, it was rebuilt into a shop pickup truck. Note the oversize headlamps and eagle topped bell. Photo courtesy Glenn Banz

The Knox air-cooled engine did fine in the wintertime, but overheated some in the summer. Note pin construction on cylinder for cooling.

In 1908, the Geo. N. Pierce Co. of Buffalo, New York, built this Fire Chief Wagon in conjunction with the Foss Hughes Motor Car Co. of Philadelphia. The machine was built for the Philadelphia Fire Department Chief, as a result of suggestions received from fire officials. The chassis was a stock Pierce-Arrow car and the body was constructed with two runabout seats and a box compartment to contain fire fighting hose and tools. Other equipment was attached to the outside of the body. It was reported to be capable of speeds up to 50 miles per hour.

The Springfield, Massachusetts Fire Department used several of these 1908 air-cooled Knox automobiles for its chiefs. It was fully equipped for its time with acetylene headlights and floodlight, Dietz Fire King lantern, fire extinguisher, and a Sterling electric siren. Chief cars were beginning to be decorated with stripes and gold leaf designs as shown.

Cameron inline four-cylinder with cast cooling fins. Note long vertical rocker arms on outside of cylinders. Photo courtesy AACA Library & Research Center

This 1908 air-cooled Cameron was built in Beverly, Massachusetts, for the Auburn, New York Fire Department. This 20-horsepower Model 8 was specially built as a fire department car. It had two seats forward and a seat for two facing to the rear. It is equipped with floodlight, fire extinguisher and lantern on a 98-inch wheelbase. The round screened front was typical of air-cooled automobiles of this era. Photo courtesy T.J. Carpenter

Fire Dep't. Chief Mooney's Auto, Bridgeport, Conn.

Bridgeport, Connecticut, was the home of the Locomobile Co. of America. Fire Chief Mooney was "right at home" with his 1908 Model E Locomobile touring car. Photo courtesy Robert Potter

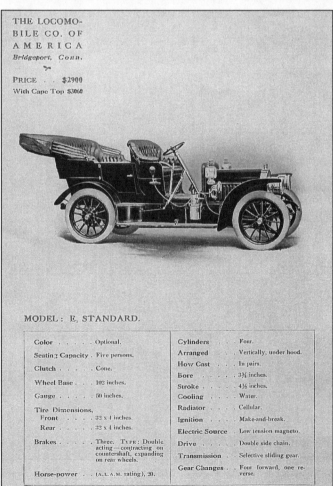

THE LOCOMO-
BILE CO. OF
A M E R I C A
Bridgeport, Conn.

PRICE . . $2900
With Cape Top $3060

MODEL : E, STANDARD.

Color	Optional.	Cylinders . .	Four.
Seating Capacity .	Five persons.	Arranged . . .	Vertically, under hood.
Clutch	Cone.	How Cast . . .	In pairs.
Wheel Base . . .	102 inches.	Bore	3¾ inches.
Gauge	56 inches.	Stroke	4½ inches.
Tire Dimensions,		Cooling	Water.
Front	32 x 4 inches.	Radiator	Cellular.
Rear	32 x 4 inches.	Ignition	Make-and-break.
Brakes	Three. Type: Double acting — contracting on countershaft, expanding on rear wheels.	Electric Source .	Low tension magneto.
		Drive	Double side chain.
		Transmission . .	Selective sliding gear.
Horse-power . . .	(A.L.A.M. rating), 30.	Gear Changes . .	Four forward, one reverse.

The Most Reliable American Car

The 1908 Locomobile Car is a highly refined development of the type which we first manufactured in 1902. It is a combination of exceedingly strong components, reliability being the foremost consideration, and skilful designing, coupled with the use of the best and most appropriate materials, results in a structure of moderate weight and maximum durability.

¶ Locomobile cars have always enjoyed an unrivaled reputation for reliability and freedom from road troubles, and this is due to the fact that we have maintained the highest manufacturing ideals, building each car as *well* and *thoroughly* as we could. Every year we have produced a limited number of the highest quality cars ; every year our product has advanced in merit and reputation. In 1908 we shall continue our past policy, both as to quality and general design, but we believe that our new models will give increased satisfaction, even greater than the splendid, *trustworthy* cars heretofore produced.

¶ Two cars will be manufactured, type "E," 20 h. p., and type "I," 40 h. p. The type "E" Locomobile is the development of a model brought out in 1905 and manufactured ever since ; the type "I" Locomobile resembles the 1907 type "H," only having a motor of largely increased power.

THE *Locomobile* COMPANY
OF AMERICA
FACTORY: BRIDGEPORT, CONN.
BRANCH OFFICES
New York, Broadway and 76th Street   Boston, 400 Newbury Street
Philadelphia, 245 N. Broad Street   Chicago, 1354 Michigan Avenue
Member Association of Licensed Automobile Manufacturers.

Specifications for the Locomobile.

This is as simple as it gets! No bells or sirens, just one big placard. Photo courtesy Ed Haas collection

Parade-ready fire fighters in Tulsa, Oklahoma, and their 1909 Chalmers-Detroit chemical-equipped fire chief runabout. This 40-horsepower four-cylinder car cost $2,750, f.o.b. Detroit. Photo courtesy Steve Loftin collection

This 1910 Mitchell Chief's car was a gift to the Racine Fire Department from the Mitchell Car Co. of Racine, Wisconsin. It was valued at $1,500. This four-cylinder 30-horsepower touring car was the first motorized vehicle for the department. The man in the suit is Chief James Cape. The Mitchell was destroyed in a wreck on Christmas eve 1914, when the driver took it on a joyride. "Silent as the foot of time" was the Mitchell slogan. Photo courtesy Racine Firebell Museum Association.

A 1910 Overland runabout was the first motorized Chief's car for the Toledo, Ohio Fire Department. This popular Model 38 with a four-cylinder 25-horsepower engine performed so well that the Overland Co. advertised that it would carry four people up a 45 percent grade from a standing start. Note the height of the carbide headlamps and the front mounted bell. The box top in the rear was fitted with a seat and handrails for passengers. Cost $1,000. Photo courtesy Toledo Firefighters Museum

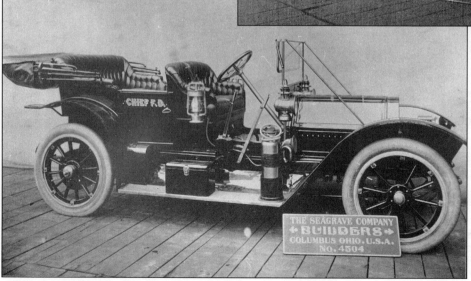

The Seagrave Co. assembled a few chief cars with parts from the Frayer-Miller Co. of Springfield, Ohio. The #5129 roadster was sold to Piedmont, California, and the #4504 touring car was delivered to New Orleans, Louisiana, c.1910. These are two of the few factory photographs of a chief car, taken on the loading dock at the Seagrave factory. #4504 photograph was taken with a white canvas background. Photos courtesy Matt Lee

The Carter Motor Car Co. built this 1910 Washington Chief car for the District of Columbia Fire Department. Chief Wagner is seated beside his aide and driver, Pvt. Moxley. The windshield was later removed and a bell installed on the dashboard equipped with a Klaxon noise machine. The beautiful building in the background is the firehouse for Engine #2 at 12th NW, and still stands today. Photo courtesy Jackson Gerhart collection

The first motorized Chief's car in Scranton, Pennsylvania, was this 1910 Buick Model 17. It had a 318-cubic inch four-cylinder engine, rated at 32.4 horsepower, and weighed 2,790 pounds. Chief Henry F. Ferber is seated right front. This skillfully decorated machine has dashboard-mounted floodlight, three-gallon extinguisher, Dietz lanterns, two spare tires and a front bumper. Photo courtesy Mark Boock

The City of Richmond, Virginia, placed in service its first motorized apparatus in 1911. Included with the order from the Knox Automobile Co. were three Chief cars, including this Tourabout model. By 1910, all Knox vehicles were water cooled. Lettering on the hood designates Chief. The car is equipped with hand crank siren and searchlight. Photo courtesy Tom Herman collection

Another of the three Richmond, Virginia, Chief cars ordered from the Knox Automobile Co., this also being a Tourabout model. Lettering on the hood designates 2nd Asst. Chief. The car is equipped with hand crank siren, searchlight, extinguisher and lantern. Note horses are still part of the fire scene in 1911. Photo courtesy Tom Herman collection

Chief Engineer George Cushing and his driver, Burt Brown, pose with this 1910 Knox Chemical Chief's Wagon from Hingham, Massachusetts. The Knox Co. manufactured many of the early motorized apparatus for fire departments. Photo courtesy The Bare Cove Fire Museum

A postcard picture of a c.1910 Pope Hartford roadster, from Kansas City, Missouri. The body seating is for two passengers like a 1910 model, but the electric headlights and cowl lights may be from a later model. Note the custom radiator script for the fire department. Photo courtesy Glimpse of Time.

This 1911 Speedwell four-door Toy Tonneau is from our neighbors north of the border in Vancouver, B.C. Chief Carlisle is shown with his driver. This nicely decorated white car was powered by a 50-horsepower four-cylinder engine. Cost $2,700. Top and windshield extra. Note trumpet of warning device mounted through the lower windshield, and empty double spare tire brackets. Photo courtesy Alex Matches

Factory photo from Knox Automobile Co. showing Body Type H mounted on a Model "R" Chief's car. Price included one three-gallon extinguisher, headlights, searchlight, locomotive bell, speedometer, horn and tools: $3,150. Power was a four-cylinder 40-horsepower engine and the standard paint color was Mercedes Red. Photo courtesy AACA Library & Research Center

Chief Fraser

Chief George W. Fraser behind the wheel of Toledo's rumble roadster c.1910 Overland Chief's car. This later model has a Prest-O-Lite tank for lamps and an early Klaxon. Photo courtesy Toledo Firefighters Museum

A 1911 photograph of Chief Engineer Charles "Chick" Highham and his Buick roadster of the Middletown, New York Fire Department. It looks like a racer, and Buick was winning automobile races with cars equipped with engines over 300 cubic inches during this time. The rear mounted 27-gallon gas tank increased the distance between fuel stops. Photo courtesy A.H. Still/Marvin Cohen

EXPANDING MOTORIZATION ERA: 1911-1919

By the end of the 20th century's first decade, the interest in motorized Chief vehicles was developing along with equal enthusiasm for the new motorized apparatus. The expanding use factors experienced by the large city departments was a wake-up call for many other cities and suburban fire companies that protected large areas. The largest turnout of fire chiefs in history occurred at the 1909 Fire Chief Convention. It was held in Grand Rapids, Michigan, close to our nation's automotive industrial center.

More than 550 fire chiefs came to see and learn about the new "machines." They saw pumping and chemical apparatus built on automobile chassis. They listened to the testimony of other fire service officers, about how valuable the automobile had become, especially covering large areas and longer distances than horses. The motorization in the early years had proven itself, and the word was out! The reaction from a large number of the attending Chiefs was quite clear, when orders for automobiles were filled during the Teen years.

Reliability improvements were made to electrical systems, including the self-starter feature. Many small departments purchased Model T Ford chassis and an add-on package of chemical and hose equipment. Some built their own affordable apparatus body or ordered a factory runabout for a Chief car and added tools and fire extinguishers. A trend to left-hand drive and bigger engines affected the large city departments, such as New York and Detroit, which were busy purchasing multi-orders of Chief cars from proven manufacturers. Chiefs were motorizing with names such as: Ford, Chevrolet, Buick, Cadillac, Knox, Pierce-Arrow, Peerless, Studebaker, Chalmers, White, Stutz, and Reo. Some of these manufacturers were also building heavier apparatus for the same fire departments. Nickel plating on apparatus and automobiles became popular. The Chief and fire officials were weighing the eight to ten miles per gallon at twelve cents per gallon against the price of "oats," and the gasoline was winning. Although electric and steam cars were tried, and diesel engines were later introduced, gasoline would remain the fuel of choice for automobiles the rest of the century.

The fire department apparatus and Chief's car of Findlay, Ohio, are mustered in front of their firehouse for this group photograph. This was a typical scene in the expanding motorization period of the Teens. The horses shared their quarters with the motorized apparatus during this transition era. Chief Charles M. Arthur and his Findlay-built 1916 Grant are parked beside a 1913 Adams fire apparatus also built in Findlay by the Adams Bros. Co. Photo courtesy William W. Phillips

This Newport News, Virginia Fire Department "portrait" includes the Chief and his c.1916 Dodge Brothers touring car. This department was fully motorized by the mid-Teens with (L-R) an American LaFrance, Seagrave, and South Bend apparatus. Photo courtesy William Killen

The Chiefs of the Detroit, Michigan Fire Department in their new 1911 Cartercars. The Cartercar second from right was purchased in 1906 and the last one in line in 1907. These two cars were continually in service, and provided proof that they were reliable. They were built in Detroit until the company moved to nearby Pontiac in 1907. All of the new cars shown are Model H, 30-horsepower runabouts with a friction transmission. Mr. Carter believed the number of drive speeds should be the choice of the driver, not his car's transmission. Bells and windscreens are mounted on all the new cars. Photo courtesy Walter McCall

FDNY 1911 Model T Ford cruising the bricks of a New York City street. Photo courtesy the Mand Library & Research Center of New York

1911 photograph of FDNY Fire Commissioner Waldo (in suit), in a Model T Ford runabout. Photo courtesy AACA Library & Research Center

Ten Model Ts purchased in 1911 for FDNY Division Chiefs. These bright red runabouts were equipped with identical equipment. Each had a mounted rocker-type locomotive bell and a small box on the back for tools and rope or other small items. Each car also had an inflated spare tire, in case of tire trouble. Photo courtesy AACA Library & Research Center

This pair of 1911 Rambler roadsters were Chief cars of the Sacramento, California Fire Department. They were powered by 34-horsepower four-cylinder gas engines. The 112-inch wheelbase car cost $2,105. Photo courtesy Pioneer Mutual Hook & Ladder Society

These four McLaughlin Chief cars appeared on the back cover of a Vancouver Firemen's Benefit Association souvenir booklet in 1911. This McLaughlin endorsement shows the Toronto FD Chief's car (upper left), Vancouver FD Chief's car with Chief Carlisle (upper right), Vancouver FD Asst. Chief's car with Asst. Chief Thompson (lower left), and Victoria FD Chief's car (lower right). Photo courtesy Alex Matches

Passaic, New Jersey Fire Department used this 1911 Buick Model 21 to carry its Chief Officers: (L-R) Captain Spencer Peal, Master Mechanic and Driver William Coffey, and Chief Reginald Bowrer in front of fire headquarters. Buick produced 3,000 Model 12s in 1911 for $1,550 apiece. Photo courtesy Ernest Rodrigues collection

This c.1912 Glide Chief's car served the Vancouver (B.C.) Fire Department. The two-passenger scout cost $2,000, was self-starting, and was powered by a 45-horsepower four-cylinder engine. In the passenger seat is Deputy Chief Thompson. Photo courtesy Alex Matches

Chief Robert O. Mesnar, a 66-year veteran of the Canton, Ohio Fire Department, is in the passenger seat of this 1912 Chalmers Six Model 12 Chief's car. The Chalmers was painted gray, which was the color of all the Canton apparatus until 1931. It was reported that Chief Mesnar did not like red. This car had a 130-inch wheelbase and is equipped with a "Reiter" gong, made in Canton, and Babcock extinguisher. This photograph was taken during or after World War I, because of the USA gas rationing sticker on the windshield. Photo courtesy Bill Woodring/ Tim Elder

Chief Shewsbury is at the wheel of this 1912 Mitchell Combination Chemical Chief car from Long Beach, California. He was killed in 1916 driving this car to a fire when he collided with other fire apparatus from the same department. Note the extra chemical container on the runningboard. Photo courtesy Long Beach Fire Museum

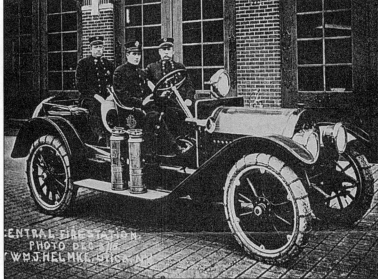

This c.1912 Cadillac served the Utica, New York Fire Department as the first motorized Chief's rig. (L-R) Deputy Chief Frank Breitenberg, Driver Walter Monroe, and Chief Daniel J. Sullivan. This car was equipped with a Delco electric starting, ignition, and lighting system, searchlight included. A Sterling siren and fire extinguishers are part of the first "rig." Tire chains on all four wheels was for safety. The advancement of electrical equipment on automobiles set the stage for accessories. Photo courtesy William Cary

St. Louis purchased this 1912 American Traveler from the American Motors Co. of Indianapolis, for Chief Swingley (passenger front seat). This Model 54 touring car had a 124-inch wheelbase underslung chassis. It was advertised that the underslung prevented the car from turning "turtle," safely ten degrees more than other cars. Safety was starting to show in cars with enclosed bodies and lower frame and seating design. Photo courtesy Glenn Banz

The white colored c.1912 McLaughlin runabout was the first Chief's car for Point Grey, B.C. Photo courtesy Alex Matches

This 1912 EMF-Studebaker was a Model 30 roadster serving Boise, Idaho. Chief Harry Fulton and Driver Fulmer have no protection from the wind, but the car's radiator is shielded from the cold. This 30-horsepower four-cylinder car was equipped with electric lights and self-starter. Cost $1,100. A Babcock extinguisher is on board. The Studebaker Co. took over EMF (Everitt, Metzger, and Flanders) completely by 1912. Photo courtesy Scott Schimpf collection

Fleet of Chief's Roadsters owned by the City of Yonkers, New York

Orange, New Jersey

Akron, Ohio

Macon, Georgia

Montgomery, Alabama

Cleveland, Ohio

Chief's Car with Chemical Tank and Hose Reel

This gallery of c.1912 White Chief cars is a sampling of the production of the White Co. of Cleveland, Ohio. The company ended automobile production in 1918, but continued to build trucks, including many fire apparatus. Photo courtesy Paul Romano collection

The Chief of the Green Bay, Wisconsin Fire Department used this c.1913 White chemical car for quick response. This four-cylinder car had a Sterling siren for its warning device beside the matching color bulb horn. The hose box and extra chemical charge supported the chemical tank operation. Photo courtesy Paul Romano collection

This c.1913 White Chief's car had a six-cylinder engine, rated at 60 horsepower. This four-passenger roadster carried the Chief Engineer of Philadelphia, Pennsylvania. Note the size of the bell! Photo courtesy Paul Romano collection

Columbus, Ohio, purchased this fleet of Firestone-Columbus machines in 1912. The four-door, seven-passenger touring car was based on a 122-inch wheelbase chassis, with left-hand steering and electric lights. This squad car is the only one with a bell. The three Chief cars are "Vis-A-Vis" Torpedo Model 78D on a 108-inch wheelbase. Firestone-Columbus production ended in 1914. Photo courtesy AACA Library & Research Center

Passaic, New Jersey Fire Department used this Model T Ford for the Asst. Chief car. Asst. Chief Walter Gibson is at the wheel. Note the single seat bucket in back and a Klaxon noise machine on the apron pan. Steering is changing from right to left. Photo courtesy Ernest Rodrigues collection

This unusual Chief's car is from South Vancouver, B.C. Fire Chief Clark is shown in both views, one with the car's top up and the other with it folded. This sharp vee radiator automobile is a 1913 Abbott-Detroit Model 44-50 Battleship Roadster. Note the rows of extended fasteners used on the steel metal body. Cost $1,250. A Sterling siren and side light is mounted up front in one picture only. Note the extra large extinguisher. A 1924 license plate in the group photo indicates the car is eleven years old, and has lived up to its name "The Battleship." Photos courtesy Alex Matches collection

This 1913 Stutz roadster was built in Indianapolis, Indiana, for the fire department of Indianapolis. Lettering indicates it was used by the Battalion Chief of District No. 4. The 120-inch wheelbase car was powered by a 60-horsepower four-cylinder T-head Wisconsin engine. Cost $2,000. Stutz retained its right-hand drive until 1922. Note double headed white arrows on tires. Photo courtesy Roger Birchfield collection

Courtesy AACA Library & Research Center

Ahrens-Fox, one of the great apparatus manufacturers, built four Model E-C Chief roadsters in 1913 hoping to capture the Chief car sales in cities that purchased Ahrens-Fox fire apparatus. It failed. Two had chemical tanks as shown. The chassis were built by Republic Automobile Co. of Hamilton, Ohio. They were powered by a 44-horsepower six-cylinder engine. The entire production stayed in Cincinnati, used by the four district fire marshals. Photo courtesy Keith Marvin

This Protective Department roadster for Boston, Massachusetts, was a 1913 White. Superintendent Sam Abbott has five stripes on his coat sleeves. Each "hash mark" denotes five years of service. The car is well-equipped with electric lights, bumper, rear toolbox with cushion and handrail for extra seating, and an electric siren. The taillamp is mounted sideways, in order to use the red side lens. The only marking on the car is the small monogram on the door (BPD). Photo courtesy of Bill Noonan

This early-1913 Willys Overland Model 71 Chief's car from the Toledo, Ohio Fire Department has a different type of bell fronting the radiator. It has an electric coil under the bell shape cover, which activates the ball end striker against the gong. A locomotive-type bell above also clears the roadway. Note the runningboard tool compartment that made for a higher first step. Chief Mayo (passenger seat) and his driver, Dan Carroll are pictured.

The original file card on the Willys Overland Model 71 Chief's car. Note the locomotive bell and electric bell are lined out because they were not purchased with this car, but transferred from the previous Chief's car. Note the sale price of $35.00 in 1925.

Boston (Massachusetts) District Chief Sennott used this 1914 four-cylinder Buick roadster. The bell is mounted on a wishbone bracket in front of radiator. Photo courtesy Ernest Rodrigues collection

Another 1914 Buick from Boston, Massachusetts. Acting District Chief Albert Caulfield used car 3 assigned to Fort Hill Square station. It has the same wishbone bell mounting. Note the novel "blackwall" Goodyear cord tires. Photo courtesy Bill Noonan

A 1914 Velie roadster with Chief Hawk at the wheel. M.F.D. lettering on the door relates to the Moline Fire Department of Illinois. Moline was the home of the Velie Co. from 1908-1928. Again, a local car manufacturer won the approval of the protecting fire department. Note the large plated bell and the fire extinguisher.

Indianapolis, Indiana, was home to more than 70 different car manufacturers over the years. In 1914, a Cole two-passenger roadster was selected for the city's 2nd Asst. Chief's car. This 28.9-horsepower four-cylinder car had electric headlights and starting. Cost $1,925. It looks like the Chief can't let go of his horse! Photo courtesy AACA Library & Research Center

This 1914 Buick roadster was the first Chief's car in Winston-Salem, North Carolina. Chief Harry E. Nissen and his driver, Lum Shore are sitting in front of Station No. 1 on South Liberty Street near Old Salem. Nissen was Chief until his death in 1932, when he was killed driving his Hudson roadster to a fire and collided with a bus. Photo courtesy Steve Cloutier collection

Winston-Salem's Station No. 1 as photographed in 1998.

1914 photograph of the delivery of four new Model "K" Willys Knight roadsters to the Toledo, Ohio Fire Department headquarters on Jefferson Ave. These Chiefs' cars were built in the former Garford Plant at Elyria, Ohio, with the new Knight Sleeve Valve engine. In 1915, Willys integrated all production into this Toledo complex. The Toledo Fire Department records on these cars are included. Photo and records courtesy Toledo Firefighters Museum

This 1915 Buick is a Model C-55 four-door touring car. Chief John Mullen of the Boston Fire Department and his driver, Charles Cosgrove are posed in the front seat of this new style body. The Buick was powered by a 55-horsepower six-cylinder overhead valve engine. This new overhead valve design permitted lower compression with better shaped combustion chambers. Cost $1,650. Buick was a major manufacturer during the Teens, producing 42,000 units in 1915, which jumped to 124,000 in 1916. Note the wishbone mounted bell and front BFD tag used on all Boston Fire Department cars until the 1950s. Photo courtesy Bill Noonan collection

The Ford Motor Co. was also setting new production records with Model T sales of 300,000 units in 1915. The city of Alexandria, Virginia, purchased this car for Chief Kenneth Ogden, shown with his driver, Charles Jones. The Model T is equipped with a Sterling siren, battery-type lantern, searchlight, and fire extinguisher. Photo courtesy Mrs. Kenneth Ogden and Ashton McKenney collection

This 1915 Marmon four-passenger touring car is fitted with an Eagle on the front-mounted bell. Chief Frank Henderson of the St. Louis, Missouri Fire Department took delivery in July 1915 at a cost of $3,250. This picture was taken before 1917, when the new Chief, William G. Pauzer ordered the white car to be painted red. It was sold in 1925. Photo courtesy Glenn Banz collection

This Chief's car is a 1915 Lewis VI touring. It was powered by a 60-horsepower six-cylinder engine. Cost $750. It served the Racine Fire Department of Racine, Wisconsin. (L-R) Chief James Cope, the driver, Captain William Butterfield, Charles Jefferson, and Fire Alarm Electrician, John Sisco. The Lewis slogan was "Monarch of the Sixes." Photo courtesy Racine Firebell Museum Association

This is the first motorized Chief's "Buggy" for Rome, New York. It's a 1915 Oldsmobile touring car equipped with a bell, Dietz lanterns and two fire extinguishers. Photo courtesy William Cary collection

This 1915 Speedwell Chief's car is pictured between other apparatus serving the Vancouver (B.C.) Fire Department. Built in Dayton, Ohio, this 41-horsepower six-cylinder car was built on a 135-inch wheelbase chassis. The Speedwell Co. declared bankruptcy early in 1915. Photo courtesy Alex Matches

A 1915 Peerless Chief's car serving Canton, Ohio. Asst. Chief Schario is standing beside the driver. Note the large gong for the warning device. Peerless automobiles were built in nearby Cleveland, Ohio, until 1931. Photo courtesy Tim Elder collection

A 1916 photograph taken in Boston, Massachusetts, of District No. 1 Chief's car after it hit a streetcar. The knicker crowd is surveying the damage to the 1914 Buick roadster. A combination of two wheel brakes, smooth tires, and wet streetcar tracks caused a lot of accidents involving Chief cars racing to fires. Photo courtesy Bill Noonan

This 1916 Dodge Chief's car is pictured with a quilted blanket covering the hood and radiator. The roadster has its doors monogrammed for the city of Detroit, Michigan Fire Department. This small car weighed 2,155 pounds and cost $785 with electric lights and a self-starter. Bumpers and spare tire were optional. Note the rearview side mirror! Also note the massive wrought iron hinges on the firehouse doors! Photo courtesy Matt Lee

Yes, Model T Fords were everywhere. This typical runabout weighed 1,395 pounds and cost $390 in 1916. Over 98,000 runabouts were built that year. This picture was taken in 1917 during World War I, and this Chief was showing his patriotism with the U.S. flag in the windshield. Photo courtesy Scott Schimpf

This Chief car is a 1916 Grant Model V roadster built in Findlay, Ohio, for the Findlay Fire Department. A light car powered by a 22-horsepower six-cylinder engine. Cost $795. A Sterling electric siren and a fire extinguisher are attached to the left runningboard. Photo courtesy William W. Phillips

The District of Columbia Fire Department's Battalion Chief and his driver aide are ready to roll! This 1916 Jeffery roadster, made in Kenosha, Wisconsin, was powered by a 40-horsepower four-cylinder engine. A Klaxon noise machine clears the street. Note the battery-operated lantern with the waterproof case has replaced the standard Deitz oil lantern. Photo courtesy Jackson Gerhart collection

This 1916 Reo roadster served the Fire Chief of Harrisburg, Pennsylvania, for many years. An early model Sterling siren cleared the roadway. Runningboard mountings were common for stand-up fire extinguishers. The building in the background is the John Harris Mansion, home of the city's founder. It became the Dauphin County Historical Society's home, and is now open to the public. Photo courtesy David Houseal collection

A Deputy Chief from Cambridge, Massachusetts, stands beside his 1917 Buick roadster. The bell mounting is similar to the wishbone-type used in Boston. Cost of the Buick was $985 with a six-cylinder overhead valve engine.

This 1923 photograph shows wear-and-tear on this 1917 Cadillac chief's car from Hyattsville, Maryland. Chief John Fainter has the rumbleseat open and top up on a sunny day. Engines were getting bigger in the late-Teens and this Cadillac was no exception with a 314.5-cubic inch L-head V-8. Cost new, $2,240. Fire equipment includes electric siren, searchlight on a runningboard mount, and fire extinguisher. Front bumper and fender-mounted rearview mirror were added safety accessories. The cowl vent was a popular feature and continued on many cars into the 1950s. Photo courtesy Steve Cloutier

May 10, 1919, a photographer in Scranton, Pennsylvania, recorded this aftermath between a two-ton tow truck and this Chief's car. An Asst. Chief and three other firemen were injured in the accident. The c.1916 Stutz touring car was a Bulldog Special. Wet pavement and narrow tires (in this case, unmatched front tires) caused accidents when responding to alarms with speed. Photo courtesy of Mark Boock

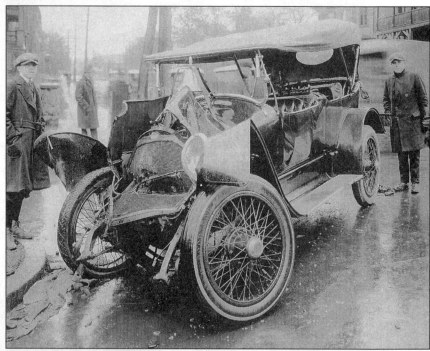

What better Chief's car to close out the decade than a 1919 Ford Model T roadster. Records show that the Ford Motor Co. had built over half of the automobiles in the world by 1919! This Toledo, Ohio, Chief's car with District Chief August Keller at the wheel was just one of the millions of cars that Henry Ford sold. The fire department records show this 22-horsepower car #10 cost $524.54. The extra equipment (wire wheels, spare tire and tube) cost $238.50. The siren cost $22.93 for a total of $785.97. The car was sold July 23, 1925, to P.S. Flanagan for $100.00. Photo courtesy Toledo Firefighters Museum

ROARING TWENTIES: 1920-1929

As the 1920s began, most city fire departments were completely motorized and even the hand-me-down companies were driving second-generation Chief cars. Many of the cities had celebrations by having "The Last Alarm" for the horses. With the whole city population on the street, the fire alarm would be sounded and the team run out of the station, at a gallop, allowing the people to cheer on the horses for the last time. At the same time, the new motorized apparatus was housed. The first Chief cars were being placed in reserve when new cars were delivered. Reserve cars were then reassigned to the shops and lighter duties, or just sold outright.

New pumping apparatus was replacing the chemical wagons as well as the original automobile-type chassis hose wagons.

Motorized fire apparatus sales took a slight dip during a brief depression in 1920-21, but recovered, along with the automobile industry, to a new high in 1927-28. The 1929 Great Depression changed the fire department automobile brands forever. The former loyalty to hometown makes of automobile was gone. Many of the famous name automobiles purchased in the Teens would be out of business by the end of the "crash" decade. Locomobile, Moon, Cole, Jordan, Stutz, and Marmon are a few of the 181 manufacturers in 1922 that vanished or were "near death" by the end of 1929. Name changes were also typical of this period. By the end of the Great Depression, three major car companies would emerge as General Motors, Ford Motor Co., and Chrysler Corp. Hudson, Nash, Studebaker, Packard, and Willys Overland would stay independent and compete with the "Big Three" for several decades.

Fire departments, with few exceptions, continued to purchase open runabouts and touring cars for their Chief Officers into the middle-1920s. The common belief that the open cab apparatus was necessary, carried over to the Chief's car for many years. By 1924, the wood-reinforced bodies diminished in popularity, and body manufacturers were starting to construct all-steel bodies. This design improvement, along with the introduction of safety glass, created the greatest accident-protection advance made during the 1920s. Fire officials realized the advantages of a closed car, and coupes and sedans were starting to show up on the equipment rosters. The invention of the engine thermostat put the hot water heaters in closed cars. Now the Chief's car had become a haven from the cold and windy weather. Another item we take for granted today is the windshield wiper. A vacuum motor to operate the wipers was introduced during the 1920s as a safety feature, so both hands could be kept on the steering wheel. These vacuum motors were used into the 1950s, finally replaced by an electric motor that didn't have the problem of vacuum loss during acceleration.

The 1920s also saw the invention of ethyl gasoline, which improved engine performance and helped prevent vapor lock. Hydraulic brakes replaced mechanical brakes for safer stops. Steel disc wheels replaced spoke wheels, and balloon tires changed the ride and handling and gave the driver more rubber on the road.

All of these factors helped improve the usefulness and safety of the Chief's car during the roaring Twenties.

This late-1920s Oldsmobile is typical of the changing scene of fire departments all over the nation during this decade. This firehouse in Clifton, New Jersey, is fully motorized with a 1924 Ahrens-Fox pumper and 1924 Ahrens-Fox aerial ladder truck. Note the solid rubber tires. Photo courtesy Ernest Rodrigues collection

Boston, Massachusetts, had lots of Buick cars for its officers. Shown is Captain Charles Springer, acting District Chief, in a 1920 Model K-44 roadster. This 60-horsepower overhead valve car cost $1,495. Photo courtesy Bill Noonan

CHIEF'S CAR HELD UP *1920 May 5* TILL FLAG IS PAINTED

Just because the Daniels company didn't have a man in its painting department who could paint the flag of Scranton on the hood of the machine as specified Superintendent of Fires Peter J. Rosar did not get the new department car yesterday. The machine will instead arrive here on Monday next week.

The car was entirely finished, and prepared for shipment, when it was found the flag of the city couldn't be put on, and it became necessary to send the hood to Philadelphia, where a frescoer was put to work on the job. The machine is to replace the old Stutz, which was wrecked in a collision last year.

This bright red 1920 Daniels was manufactured in Reading, Pennsylvania, for Superintendent of Fires Peter J. Rosar of Scranton, Pennsylvania, but was delivered late because it lacked a flag (see inset). The touring body was made from aluminum, yet the car weighed three tons! This Model D developed 90-horsepower from a 404-cubic inch V-8 that gave it a world of power for climbing hills. It also had a cast pewter radiator shell. Cost $4,500. Note the booster nozzle mounted on the runningboard. Photo courtesy Mark Boock

1920 Peerless Model 56 touring car from Canton, Ohio. Chief R.O. Mesnar with the white cap stands beside his ride. Note the height of that running-board! It brings the fire extinguisher up to a nice arms length, but watch that first step! Photo courtesy Tim Elder collection

This 1926 photograph shows a 1920 Stutz, the second "buggy" for the Asst. Chief of Indianapolis, Indiana. It replaced a 1912 Stutz and was later replaced with a 1929 Stutz roadster. Fire equipment includes a center cowl red light and Sireno Type 7 siren, clapper bell and battery-operated hand light. Photo courtesy Roger Birchfield collection

A formal picture of Chief John B. Gordon and his 1920 Chandler touring car when purchased. Haverhill is 32 miles north of Boston, Massachusetts. The Chandler is equipped
with a bell, two Deitz Fire King lanterns, and two gooseneck fire extinguishers. The Court
Street Station pictured was built in 1882.

A newspaper photograph from a local paper showing Chief Gordon's Chandler on June 21,
1922. The driver, Lloyd Walker was fatally injured in the accident. His vision was blocked
by a rain covered windshield, and he leaned out the side to look and was hit on the head by
a passing electric streetcar. Wet roads and streetcars caused a lot of car accidents. Photos
courtesy C.W. Reynolds

It's doubtful that this c.1921 Oakland Chief's touring car would ever see service again. This Scranton, Pennsylvania Bureau of Fire car collided with a three-ton truck responding to a "paint shop" fire in November 1923. Asst. Chief Edmund Lewis and four firemen were hurt. Photo courtesy Mark Boock

This bright red 1921 Dorris seven-passenger touring car was in service from 1921 to 1929 in St. Louis, Missouri. A Type 6-80 six-cylinder had a 132-inch wheelbase and cost $3,995.48. The front bell helped to clear the way. The use of side curtains on touring cars made winter weather more tolerable. The Dorris Co., of St. Louis, ended production in 1925. Photo courtesy the late P.T. Nauman collection

A 1921 Cadillac used by the Asst. Fire Marshal. CFD on the hood is the marking for Chicago Fire Department. Note the four leg mounting for the bell. Large locomotive bells such as this were used on Chief cars in large cities into the 1960s. Photo courtesy Ken Little collection

1921-22 Buick roadster assigned to Chief of Battalion No. 7 in Baltimore, Maryland. The picture is full of station "ham."

Chief and onlookers only!

Buick roadster in Baltimore during a parade.

1921-22 Buick assigned to Baltimore District Chief No. 1. These roadsters cost $1,795 in 1921 and dropped to $1,495 in 1922. The bells were secured on the upper right side of the cowl and the fire extinguisher was runningboard-mounted in a can. Note the ornate stone work on the station facade. Photo courtesy Bill Snyder

Harrisburg, Pennsylvania, Fire Chief Marion Verbeke drove this 1922 Reo roadster to perform his duties for the Bureau of Fire. A small electric siren is attached to the side. Photo courtesy David Houseal collection

A 1922 Hupmobile roadster, with Chief Oscar Grab at the wheel, serving the New Rochelle, New York Fire Department. A Sterling Model 12 siren and a fire extinguisher makes it a Chief's car! Cost $1,250. Photo courtesy Harry Rosenblum

Williamsport (Pennsylvania) Fire Chief John W. Miles and his 1923 Jewett roadster. Jewett was a subsidiary of Paige-Detroit Motor Car Co. and produced this popularly priced ($995) car from 1922 to 1927. The door lettering is the only fire department modification. Photo courtesy Edward G. Frey

This Chief's 1923 Studebaker roadster serving Tulsa, Oklahoma, is sporting an aftermarket front bumper and headlights. Bow ties were the order of the day for the parade! Photo courtesy Steve Loftin collection

CLOSE-COUPLED, low-hung and with the snap and dash of the popular SPECIAL-SIX motor, this car has proved one of the most desirable roadster models ever offered by any manufacturer.

The wide, straight seat, deeply upholstered in genuine leather, provides generous room for two passengers. It is placed at the exact angle for restful all-day riding. There is an unusually spacious compartment under the rear deck for all the luggage one will want to carry.

The new all-wood steering wheel, with improved type spark and throttle control, is one of the costly SPECIAL-SIX refinements.

Individually fitted storm curtains, which open with the doors, are bound on three sides by steel rods, insuring adequate protection when the weather is inclement.

Among many other unusual features are the one-piece, rain-proof windshield with automatic windshield cleaner; built-in glare-proof visor and rear-view mirror and the attractive parking lights set in the windshield base. A tool pocket is conveniently located in the left door, which is operated with the same key that locks the ignition switch and transmission lock.

Special-Six 2-Passenger Roadster

The lines of the Roadster are enhanced by graceful fenders, the tailored top and a large plate-glass window in the one-piece rear curtain.

Sales ad for Studebaker Special Six. Note features include automatic windshield cleaner, built-in glare-proof visor and rear-view mirror. Ad courtesy AACA Library & Research Center

The California State Capital Building is the background for this trio of Sacramento Fire Department Chief cars. (L-R) a 1923 Stephens Six roadster built by the Moline Plow Co. (cost $1,345), a 1924 Cadillac Type V63 touring (cost $3,940) and a 1923 Dodge roadster (cost $850). (L-R) First Asst. Chief Patrick Hayes, Chief Engineer M.J. Dunphy, Second Asst. Chief Terence Mulligan, and Dan Browne. The Chief can also be identified by the additional buttons on his coat. Bumpers were not standard equipment and had to be added. Photo courtesy Pioneer Mutual Hook & Ladder Society and Randy Wootton

(Left) One of the 1920s bumper ads reflecting family safety to sell its brand.

Fire Chief Thurstod of Honolulu, Hawaii, is posed in front of his 1924 Packard touring car with his understudy during Boys Week. Photo courtesy Paul G. Fox

This 1924 Stutz served the Indianapolis Battalion No. 1 Chief from 1924 to 1929. The roadster has a Sireno Type 7 siren in the front, a red lens clip-on light, clapper bell, and hand lantern. The Stutz Co. may have used this photograph for an advertisement. Note the steering has moved to left-hand drive. Photo courtesy Roger Birchfield collection

Pittsburgh (Pennsylvania) Battalion Chief F. Loxterman and his driver are posed in this Durant sports roadster. The Department of Public Safety purchased several Durants for the Bureau of Fire during the early 1920s. Durant roadsters from 1921 through 1924 had only minor changes. Note the small bell on runningboard. Photo courtesy John Schmidt

Battalion Chief Fred Becket and driver James Scott in his 1924 Durant. Photo courtesy John Schmidt

This Reo Model T-6 was available from 1920 (cost $1,650) to 1926 (cost $1,395). This photograph (also on the front cover) shows the Chief and his driver, of Rome, New York, waiting patiently during a snowstorm for the photographer to take the picture. Photo courtesy William Cary collection

Model T Fords were still breaking sales records in 1924, when this red Chief's car was delivered to the U.S. Naval Academy at Annapolis, Maryland. It was equipped with a bell, chemical tanks, hose, ladder, 2-1/2 gallon extinguishers and Dietz lanterns. Several apparatus manufacturers used Model T chassis to produce this type of lightweight fire fighting machine. Photo courtesy William Killen collection

The Boston Fire Department used an elaborate bell mounting on this 1925 Buick Chief's roadster. This car is equipped with four-wheel mechanical brakes and came with four- or six-cylinder engine. Photo courtesy of Bill Noonan

This 1925 Chrysler Model B-70 roadster served the Branch-ville, Maryland Fire Department (cost $1,625). It is equipped with a Sterling siren and two spotlights with runningboard supports. The C-1 on the front plate indicates Chief. Note the gold leaf striping and painted bumper. Photo courtesy Charles Black

This c.1925 Nash roadster Chief's car was modified for airport duty, with two large tanks and a hose reel. The horizontal gas cylinder on the runningboard was used to pressurize the tanks and charge the hose line. The two-and-one-half-gallon fire extinguisher was used for small fires.

This unusual inside photograph was taken of Central Station No. 1 of Canton, Ohio, in 1925. Note the station's press tin ceiling. The 1925 Studebaker Asst. Chief's vehicle is in the foreground. Apparatus: (L-R) a 1924 Seagrave, 1922 American LaFrance, 1925 Seagrave, 1921 American LaFrance, and the Studebaker. All the vehicles are painted gray. Studebaker offered a "Navajo Grey" as an available color. Photo courtesy Tim Elder collection

Williamsport, Pennsylvania, is the home of Lycoming engines, so this 1926 Gardner four-passenger roadster was a hometown-powered Chief's car (cost $1,995). The long hood covers a Lycoming 65-horsepower eight-cylinder engine. A Sterling Model 12 siren and clip-on spotlight are added items. Photo courtesy Edward Frey

Chief of Battalion 9 used a 1926 Lincoln roadster for the Bureau of Fire in Philadelphia, Pennsylvania. This body is fitted with a side compartment door, sometimes called a "golf bag" door. A Model FL Mars light is mounted under the locomotive bell. Note the two smooth spare tires. Low pressure balloon tires were offered to car buyers as an option. They put more tire surface on the road, giving a softer ride and better braking power. Photo courtesy Scott Schimpf collection

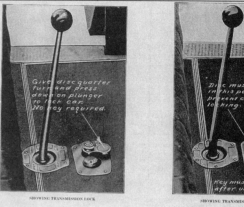

A trio of Reo Chief cars serving the capital city of Harrisburg, Pennsylvania. (L-R) a 1926 roadster with Chief Millard M. Tawney and driver Norman Arnold, 1926 roadster with 2nd Asst. Chief Arthur L. Patton and driver, and an older model roadster driven by Mechanician Raymond V. MacNeil. The balloon tires were $100 extra on the steel wheels. Note the "golf bag" door on the side. Photo courtesy the Greater Harrisburg Fire Museum

Fire Chief of Paris, Texas, showing off his 1927 Studebaker business coupe. The B&M Model CS-8 siren clears the roadway for this six-cylinder car. Two fire extinguishers mounted on the runningboard supplement the built-in chemical tank hidden in the body. The fill cap and fittings are visible behind driver's door, but no hose is showing. Photo courtesy Fred Fuston collection

This 1927 Chrysler touring car is turning out of the station with the Chief of the Salvage Corp in Baltimore, Maryland. A large bell is mounted in front and a double cell lantern is attached to the runningboard. Runningboards served as both steps and carriers. Primarily, they were attached to apparatus so firemen could safely ride to the fire instead of running alongside the apparatus, and possibly falling under the wheels. Photo courtesy Bill Snyder

The McLaughlin-Buick was "Canada's Standard Car" and this 1927 roadster was the Chief's car for the Toronto Fire Department. A Sterling siren is attached to the firewall. Note the red lens in the left headlight. Photo courtesy Walter McCall collection

A testimonial from the Fire Chief of Murphysboro, Illinois, on the use of steel tire chains for safety. The 1927 Oakland long deck roadster is also equipped with a bell, B&M Model S-8 siren, red spotlight, fire extinguisher on runningboard, and a Pyrene extinguisher on the cowl. The Pyrene Co. also made tire chains.

(Below) Artist drawing of Cadillac sedan seats and interior.

This 1927 Cadillac five-passenger sedan was used by the Fire Insurance Patrol in Chicago, Illinois. It was powered by a 314.5-cubic inch V-8 and weighed 4,270 pounds. Cost $3,250. The large bell is the only warning device. Photo courtesy Scott Schimpf

A group picture of the Chiefs and their drivers posed with the two Chief cars of the Scranton, Pennsylvania Fire Department. The car at left is a 1927 Junior Eight roadster, built by the Locomobile Co. of Bridgeport. Cost $2,150. It was powered by a 66-horsepower eight-cylinder engine. The siren is a Sterling Model 12. The car at right is a 1927 Studebaker, 75-horsepower Big Six Victoria. Cost $1,295. 1927 was Studebaker's "Diamond Jubilee" year. Its siren is a B&M. Photo courtesy of Mark Boock

Artist view of the Junior Eight roadster.

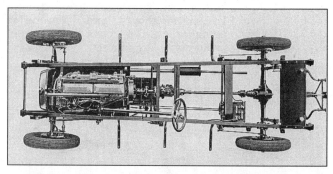

Artist view of the Junior Eight chassis with the body removed. Drawings courtesy AACA Library & Research Center

Honolulu, Hawaii Fire Department tried putting front-mounted pumps on its Chief cars. The 1928 Chevrolet had a four-cylinder engine with only 35 horsepower. These roadsters cost $500 without options or accessories. This centrifugal pump mounted to the Packard in the background would have been more satisfactory. Photo courtesy Paul G. Fox

York, Pennsylvania Fire Department had a 1928 Nash coupe for its Asst. Chief. This car was equipped with steel wheels and four-wheel mechanical brakes. The fire extinguisher and hand lantern had been standard equipment for Chief cars. A Sterling siren is cowl mounted and the large bell with eagle is mounted atop a polished pole next to the driver (sure to keep him awake with the window down!). Note the two-tone paint job. Photo courtesy York Fire Museum Archives

The two Fire Insurance cars pictured are Graham-Paige models made during the start of the Great Depression. Both are coupes, the Chief Mechanic's car is a two-passenger and the Asst. Chief's car is a two-/four-passenger. Note the two-tone paint job (black over red) that became a trademark for the Chicago, Illinois Fire Department. The bell is supported by a four leg bracket. Photos courtesy Scott Schimpf collection

The Asst. Fire Marshal and driver posed in front of this 1928 Cadillac in Chicago, Illinois. This V-8-powered coupe has a Fisher body with a 140-inch wheelbase chassis. Cost $3,295. Note the dual rear-mounted spare tires. The bell is hidden in front. Photo courtesy Ken Little collection

This unusual photograph of the Graf Zeppelin and a Chief car is perfect for closing out the "Roaring Twenties" section. The airship arrived from Japan on a three-day crossing, and landed in Los Angeles on August 26, 1929. It was on a round-the-world safety demonstration trip. This 1929 Chrysler roadster belonged to the California State Fire Warden, who was there to enforce a no-smoking zone. This six-cylinder car had built-in radiator shutters, and two side-mounted spare tires with rearview mirrors strapped on top. Note the spare fuel-oil-water containers mounted on the runningboard. No bell or siren, but plenty of signs!

A typical department photograph taken of the uniformed men before a parade or celebration. The fire department is always an important part of any community celebration. The line of rigs in front of the Dover (Ohio) Fire Station includes a horse-drawn Ahrens Steamer, 1925 Ahrens-Fox Model J-S-4, 1919 American LaFrance, and a 1929 Model A Ford roadster Chief's car. The Model A was Henry Ford's replacement for the now famous Model T. Over 15 million Model Ts were sold. The steamer was put in reserve years ago, but still sees parade duty. Note the left headlight on the vehicles have a red lens. Photo courtesy Tim Elder collection

STREAMLINE & DESIGN: 1930-1939

The stock market crash of October 1929 was felt by the small automobile manufacturers whose production had peaked. The small companies without cash flow were ripe for picking and many nameplates disappeared. The decade started with car sales dropping and factory output falling to new lows. As an example, in 1927, Chevrolet built 1,749,000 units. By 1932, production had dropped to 306,000. Packard, in 1929, built 44,285 units. By 1934, output had plunged to 6,552.

Prices of automobiles in the early-1930s were dropping, as manufacturers were busy engineering new features to boost sales. Both factors were favorable for the buying public, but few had the money to spend. The bigger city fire departments did continue to purchase automobiles for replacement, but the average departments were using cars longer. Some departments with repair shops were rebuilding and modifying old Chief cars. The hand-me-downs were recycled instead of sold. This part of our history changes for the better, after the 1932 election. President Roosevelt's "New Deal" put huge public works projects on the front burner. Cities got new firehouses, water treatment plants were built and water systems extended into the suburbs. Highways and bridges were built, all with government programs. Both the fire departments and the automobile industry were winners.

The automobile industry developed "streamlining" with bold new designs to win over the public and boost sales. All-steel bodies with built-in trunks for hiding spare tires were new. Batteries moved under the hood, and gearshift controls moved to the steering column.

Engineering departments of every car manufacturer were designing new features, also to enhance sales, with free wheeling, synchromesh transmissions, power brakes and a vacuum clutch to name a few.

More red warning lights would appear and louder sirens would be heard due to improvements in electrical systems. Radio receivers would be used, first in police cars and then supplied to the fire department. Communications would take a giant step forward with installed equipment, which would change the fire scene forever.

Indianapolis Fire Department apparatus and the Chief with his men assigned to the Headquarters building. The group photograph with the equipment is dated 1926. The three Stutz vehicles pictured were made in Indianapolis. Stutz would not survive beyond 1935. Note the shop generic squad car (second from left) has a cowl vent on an open cab car. Photo courtesy Roger Birchfield

This 1930 LaSalle Battalion No. 8 Chief's car is parked on the street in Philadelphia, Pennsylvania. The roadster was featured by LaSalle as a "Fleetchief," a name quite fitting for the job. It is equipped with a high-mounted bell over center light and siren. This model had a rumbleseat as standard equipment, along with the "golf bag" side compartment. Photo courtesy Scott Schimpf collection

A 1930 Buick roadster was used by the Battalion Chief No. 5 of the Baltimore City Fire Department. The bumper banner indicates the fire department was into sports. Photo courtesy Bill Snyder collection

This 1930 Packard phaeton was the Fire Chief's car serving Honolulu, Hawaii. It is quite a machine, sporting side wing glass and chrome side-mounted covers for the spares. The center-mounted siren and red lens fender lights help clear the way to the fire. A Seagrave pumper stands ready to parade. Photo courtesy Bob Schierle collection

A 1931 Buick Fire Chief's car with Chief Michael Clark serving Williamsport, Pennsylvania. Balloon tires had become standard, but the side mount and front and rear bumpers were optional. This model was a four-passenger coupe. The sirens were getting louder with larger motors. Photo courtesy Edward G. Frey

Philadelphia's Chief Engineer used this 1931 Lincoln LeBaron convertible roadster. The Lincoln, powered by a 120-horsepower V-8, weighed 5,070 pounds and cost $4,700. Only 275 were built, and it was the first Lincoln model with double action hydraulic shock absorbers on all four wheels, the first to have a mechanical fuel pump and also the first to have a two-barrel downdraft carburetor. This LeBaron body had a side compartment door and a rumbleseat. The Chief gave plenty of warning with the locomotive bell, the Mars FL light, and the B&M S-8 siren. Photo courtesy Scott Schimpf collection

The Chief of the Department of FDNY was assigned this 1932 Chrysler Imperial. The LeBaron custom limousine sedan was one of 32 built and weighed 5,330 pounds. Cost $3,295. The bell, red lights, and maltese plate were added accessories. Photo courtesy Jack Lerch

A 1933 Packard phaeton serving the Fire Chief in Albany, New York. Side curtains were in use and the "Flying Lady" radiator cap was in place. A car such as this carried Franklin Roosevelt to the White House! Photo courtesy Ron Bogardus

This photograph of the same car was taken after 1956 (1956 Oldsmobile in background), and the 1933 Packard has remained in service. The lettering on the rear door has been changed to Repair Shop, and the "Lady" has disappeared! The huge red light and siren are still in place. Photo courtesy Steve Loftin collection

A 1934 Pontiac two-door sedan carried the Fire Chief of Alexandria, Virginia. This 84-horsepower eight-cylinder car cost $705 with wire wheels. Photo courtesy Aston McKenney collection

The 1934 DeSoto, Series SE, was a radical new design for the Chrysler Corp. This is unit #386 of the FDNY with a locomotive bell and red light. The Airflow was built with a unit body construction and was capable of 22 miles per gallon fuel economy with a 100-horsepower six-cylinder engine. Photo courtesy Bob Schierle collection

This 1934 Buick was a seven-passenger sedan. The car weighed 4,905 pounds and cost $2,055. The maltese plate identifies the "Chief of St. Louis Fire Department." Note the extended front bumper that protects the bell, Mars light, red light, and the B&M S-8 siren. The color was described as grayish light green until 1940 when the car was painted white with gold trim. It was sold in 1941. Photo courtesy the late P.T. Nauman collection

FDNY Battalion Chiefs used 1935 Plymouths for duty. This two-door sedan cost $615, not including the optional front and rear bumpers. All Chrysler products had four-wheel hydraulic brakes. A rocker bell and maltese plate were well anchored up front, with a red light on the fender. Photo courtesy Bob Schierle collection

Twin 1935 Ford five-window coupes for the Chief and Asst. Chief of Harrisburg, Pennsylvania. Cost $520 each. Both cars are equipped with Model 12 Sterling sirens and bells. (L-R) Driver Harry Filling, Chief Edward Halbert, Asst. Chief Earl Swartz. Chief Halbert later died in the line of duty. Photo courtesy David Houseal collection

Asst. Chief Degraves and his 1936 Plymouth Model P1 coupe, from Vancouver, B.C. Plymouth used an L-head 201.3-cubic inch engine for many years in the United States, but exported cars with 170.4-cubic inch engines. The Sterling Model 20 siren has a center roof mount. Photo courtesy Alex Matches

St. Louis, Missouri Fire Department had red lights installed on all four corners at the belt line of these 1936 Chevrolet coupe Chief's cars. That's a big bell with a flying eagle top and B&M S-8 siren up front. Photo courtesy Glenn Banz collection

Baltimore, Maryland Fire Department maintained a fleet of 1936 Buicks. The locomotive bell, red light, and Sterling Model 30 siren were mounted in identical locations on all the staff cars. The Chief's modern sedan is shown in sharp contrast to the solid tire Mack Bulldog Aerial in the background.

This black 1936 Buick Limited eight-passenger sedan was used as a departmental car. The plate indicates D-1. It was used for fire department dress uniform details, such as funerals and honor guards. Cost $1,845 with a single external side mount. It weighed over two tons! Note the short whip antenna on the roof and only a single red warning light.

Baltimore District Chief's car was a 1936 Buick business coupe.

Baltimore Superintendent of Machinery used this 1936 Buick business coupe to pull a pump trailer to additional alarms. Photos courtesy Bill Snyder

The Los Angeles City Fire Department had a fleet of 1937 Buicks. Each Chief car was uniformly fitted with two red lights. Above, Battalion Chief C.H. Roraback. At right, identity of Chief and driver are unknown. Below, (L-R) driver F. Gillite; Asst. Chief T.A. Stembridge; Battalion 5 Chief R. King and driver P. Heitkamp. The Buick coupes had all-steel body construction. Photos courtesy Dale Magee

Chief Swartz and his driver posed next to a new 1937 Buick coupe delivered to the Bureau of Fire in Harrisburg, Pennsylvania. A Sterling Model 20 siren light clears the way. Photo courtesy David Houseal collection

A 1937 Chevrolet coupe that served the St. Louis, Missouri Fire Department. This 85-horsepower six-cylinder car cost $619. The flying eagle bell and the Sterling Model 30 siren were added as were the four corner lights on the belt line. Photo courtesy Glenn Banz collection

1937 Chevrolet advertisement includes Jefferson City (Missouri) Fire Chief's coupe with fire extinguisher on running-board. Ad courtesy AACA Library & Research Center

The Fire Chief of Memphis, Tennessee, rode in style with this 1937 Chrysler Imperial. The Model C-17 was the last of the Airflow design. Cost $1,610. The antenna on the roof is for the AM signal. The front bumper was extended to provide protection to the custom siren and Mars light installation. The grille was modified with a hole, so the motor of the siren could extend inside. Two spotlights were also added equipment. Photo courtesy Steve Loftin/Memphis Fire Dept.

A 1937 Oldsmobile two-door sedan serving Whittier, California. Asst. Chief A.B. Alford posed with this eight-cylinder, Fisher-bodied car (note Fisher tag on side cowl). Photo courtesy the late Glen Alton collection

A 1937 Plymouth coupe of the San Gabriel, California Fire Department with Chief H. Mann in dress uniform. The two red lights on the roof were added. Note the siren is mounted sideways on the front bumper. The two-millionth Plymouth was built in 1937. Many of those were fire or police cars. Photo courtesy the late Glen Alton collection

Asst. Chief J. Garth and a 1937 Pontiac stationed at Santa Ana, California. This DeLuxe sedan is radio equipped and has two red lights mounted on the cowl, and an extra light attached to the front bumper bracket. Note the "E" in the square on the license plate. All public vehicles in California with "E" were exempt from annual vehicle registration. Photo courtesy the late Glen Alton collection

Baltimore, Maryland Fire Department again had Buicks in service in 1938. This Battalion No. 23 Chief's coupe had the same configuration of bell, siren and light as previously noted in 1936. Buick moved the battery to a location under the hood and added coil springs to the rear suspension as design improvements. Photo courtesy Bill Snyder

This 1938 Chrysler Imperial business coupe is leaving on a call from the 7th Battalion Headquarters at 487 New Jersey Ave. NW in Washington, D.C. This Model C-19 is the first Imperial design after the Airflow was dropped. Cost $1,123. A Mars light is roof mounted. The car had a two-way radio installed. Photo courtesy Jackson Gerhart

Asst. Chief O.F. Hardman and his 1938 Dodge sedan from Santa Monica, California Fire Department. Note the two Dodge taillights used as warning lights on the roof. Cost $910. Photo courtesy the late Glen Alton collection

Chief William J. Cawker with his 1938 Pontiac coupe from Topeka, Kansas. The light on the left fender is an Akron Brass "Akrolite." This picture was taken long before we dialed "911." Photo courtesy Bob Willever

Chief Basil A. Roberts with his 1939 Studebaker Commander coupe from Inglewood, California. It had a 90-horsepower L-head six-cylinder engine and fastback body. Cost $875. Drivetrain options included: vacuum clutch, hill holder, and overdrive. Photo courtesy the late Glen Alton collection

A delivery photograph of a 1939 Chrysler ready for overseas shipment to Turkey. The Darley Co. started with a C-22 six-cylinder sedan and added a front-mounted pump, ladder and hard sleeve roof rack, along with the bell, siren, and spotlight. The Fire Chief and his crew will get to the fire together! The wide whitewalls really dress it up! Photo courtesy Walter McCall/Matt Lee

FORTY & FIGHT: 1940-1949

And then it happened: December 7, 1941; the United States was at war.

The production of cars ceased for the war effort on February 4, 1942. The tooling, dies and machinery would be stored for future use.

The first cars produced after the war were the prewar-engineered cars of the early-1940s. Cars needed by the fire service were coming from the dealers as stripped models to get the most for the community's dollar. Priority was a key word. The final years of the decade would see change to excite and lure buyers to trade their prewar wheels.

The growth of the country demanded more and broader fire protection coverage. The metro city staffs were growing and needed more automobiles. Fleet purchases were common, and smaller community police departments would share or "hand-me-down" cars to the fire departments. Those police specials had big engines and installed radios. A little lettering and a bell and presto, a Fire Chief car! In reviewing the 1940s, what appears is a mixture of full-size and fast cars.

The 1940s opened with war in part of the world. This fire station at the Naval Powder Factory at Indian Head, Maryland, saw an increase of activity, and dealt with it, with the apparatus and crew shown. (L-R) a 1940 GMC pumper, 1933 Pirsch pumper, and a 1933 Chevrolet coupe serving as the Chief's car. Cost $445. Photo courtesy William Killen collection

The Philadelphia 9th Battalion Chief arrived at this fire scene in his 1940 Dodge coupe. This restyled body with the standard Chrysler 87-horsepower six-cylinder engine cost $755. The Bureau of Fire added the Mars light on the roof and the locomotive bell. Photo courtesy Scott Schimpf

This 1940 Buick sedan was assigned to the Salvage Corps Chief in Baltimore, Maryland. Note the size of that bell! The Chief must have had salvage rights to fireboats to get a bell that huge. Photo courtesy Bill Snyder

A 1941 Buick sedan assigned to the Asst. Chief of the Rescue Squad in Toledo, Ohio. The red lights and siren are roof mounted. Photo courtesy Bob Schierle collection

The Battalion Chief drove this 1941 Ford Tudor on his duties for the Hackensack, New Jersey Fire Department. The Tudor was the most popular model sold by the Ford Motor Co. in 1941. Over 389,900 were sold. Cost $775. A Sireno Model R-2 siren light is mounted above the windshield. Note the runningboards are now covered by the door panel, eliminating any attachment of fire extinguishers or tools. Trunks had become the storage box! Photo courtesy Richard Adelman

A 1941 DeSoto sedan and the Asst. Chief A.R. Brauns from south San Francisco, California. This model had dual electric wipers, and a Fluid-Drive coupling in the driveline. Two red lights are attached in the same position as fog lights. Chief Brauns had an AM radio for his listening pleasure as well as a two-way radio with the whip antenna installed. Photo courtesy the late Glen Alton collection

A 1941 Cadillac Chief's car leading a parade in a small town in New Jersey. This picture was taken after 1955, so the Cadillac had given this fire department good service. The siren light on the fender is a Model R-2 Sireno. An early bubble light is mounted on the roof. The two round blanks below the headlights were provisions for built-in fog lights. Photo courtesy Bob Schierle collection

Fire Chief Canfield stands proudly beside his 1941 Studebaker President Eight sedan. This super deluxe car was a star for the Beverly Hills, California Fire Department. The dual red light roof mounts were common in this West Coast area. Photo courtesy the late Glen Alton collection

Haverhill, Massachusetts, received this 1942 Buick sedan after Pearl Harbor was bombed. This Model H was built after January 1, 1942, and before production stopped for the war effort on February 4, 1942. All the trim and the grille were painted because of the government ban on chrome. The bumpers were produced before January 1942. This is the first model Buick produced with the vertical bar grille, which would be Buick's signature until 1955. Chief Benjamin L. Chase and his driver Albert R. Waitt stand beside this "Painted Chief's Wagon." Photo courtesy C.W. Reynolds collection

A Battalion Chief parked this 1942 Chevrolet coupe at the right angle to view the battle damage to the right side of his car. The sticker on the windshield shows the car passed state inspection. Philadelphia Bureau of Fire installed a Model 66L Federal siren on the roof and the traditional locomotive bell up front. Photo courtesy Scott Schimpf

This 1942 Mercury sedan was one of 4,430 built before automobile production was halted in 1942. Hackensack, New Jersey Fire Department installed a Sireno Model R-2 siren light with a weathergard ring on the left fender, a spotlight, and another warning light on the roof. The door markings include a Chief insignia in addition to the lettering. Photo courtesy Richard Adelman

This 1942 Dodge sedan served the Redwood City, California Fire Department. Chief J. Lodi stands beside his prewar radio-equipped car. The Federal siren put out 115 decibels. The bottom double bar trim is missing on the rear of the front fender and the rear fender as part of the wartime "blackout" period. The new front end design for 1942 gave this model a one-piece hood for the first time, making engine compartment access easier. The fake whitewalls look flashy with the white body color, but why Nash hubcaps? Photo courtesy the late Glen Alton collection

To illustrate the growth and changes of the fire service during the period of 1941-46, a fire department was selected from an average size town (population 22,000) with a name in 14 states: Marshall, Texas.

Photo taken May 1941. Fire Chief Carl Bechtold and his men (10) stand in front of their vehicles, a 1934 American LaFrance pumper and a 1940 Ford Tudor Chief's car. Photo courtesy Shelton Hensley Family

Photo taken September 1947. Fire Chief Bechtold and Fire Marshal H.L. Allen stand in front of the two Chief cars, a 1942 Chevrolet and a 1942 Ford. The manpower has doubled (21) and the apparatus number has grown to eight! Note the other changes: the Dr. Pepper sign and the overlapping tree are gone, and all the men are now wearing ties! Photo courtesy Fire Marshal Bill Elliott

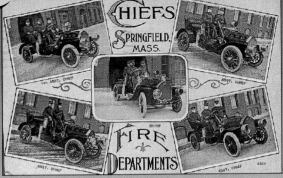

Chiefs, Springfield, Massachusetts Fire Dept.
(Knox automobiles). Courtesy Paul Romano

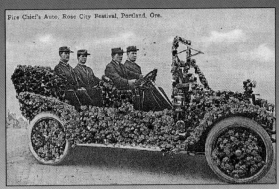

Fire Chief's auto, Rose City Festival, Portland,
Oregon. Courtesy Robert Potter

Chief Mooney's auto, Bridgeport, Connecticut Fire
Dept. (1908 Locomobile). Courtesy Louis E. Nelson

Chief, Harrisburg, Pennsylvania Fire Dept.
(1913 Studebaker). Courtesy Paul Romano

Moody Street Fire Station, Waltham, Massachusetts.
(First motorized). Courtesy Paul Romano

Fire hall, Vancouver, B.C., Canada.
(1907 Buick with new Seagrave apparatus).
Courtesy Alex Matches

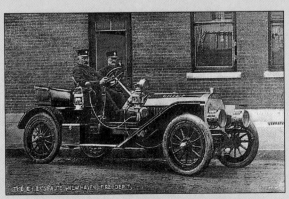

Chief's auto, New Haven, Connecticut Fire Dept.
(1909 Columbia). Courtesy Paul Romano

Grand Island Fire Dept., Grand Island, Nebraska.
(Fully motorized). Courtesy Ed Peterson

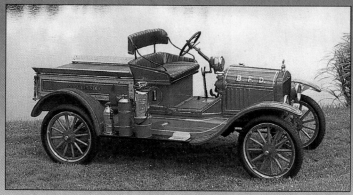

1922 Ford Model T, restored and owned by W. Parker Browne of Wooster, Ohio. Photo courtesy W. Parker Browne

A rare sight of restored Ford Chief cars. (L-to-R) 1963 owned by Steve Cloutier, Weddington, North Carolina; 1953 owned by Wayne Kidd, Mechanicsville, Virginia; 1935 owned by the Pierce Manufacturing Co., Appleton, Wisconsin. Photo courtesy Wayne Kidd

1953 Ford two-door sedan from St. Augustine Fire Dept., St. Augustine, Florida. Photo courtesy John Schmidt

1935 Ford five-window coupe replicated as a Chicago "Buggy." Owned by Howard L. Brenner, Riverwoods, Illinois. Photo courtesy Howard L. Brenner

1957 Chevrolet Bel Air Chief's wagon, Elrama Volunteer Fire Co., Elrama, Washington County, Pennsylvania. Dual Federal sirens on fenders and whitewall tires. Photo Courtesy Scott Schimpf

1965 Dodge Custom 880 four-door hardtop provided for the Chief of the Albany Fire Dept., Albany, New York. Photo courtesy Steve Loftin

1968 Ford Custom sedan carries plate No. 1 for the Chief of the District of Columbia Fire Dept. Photo courtesy Scott Schimpf

Five 1953 Buick "Special" sedans delivered to the Toledo Fire Dept., Toledo, Ohio. Photo courtesy Toledo Firefighters Museum

1989 Chevrolet Blazer provided for the 2nd Battalion Chief of San Francisco Fire Dept., San Francisco, California. Photo courtesy Bill Egan

1983 Chevrolet Caprice Classic station wagon for the Chief of the Plattsmouth Volunteer Fire Dept., Plattsmouth, Nebraska. Photo courtesy Steve Loftin

1987 AMC Eagle station wagon used by a Deputy Chief of the Pittsburgh Bureau of Fire, Pittsburgh, Pennsylvania. Photo courtesy John Schmidt

1990 Ford Crown Victoria sedan provided for 7th Battalion Chief, Kansas City Fire Dept., Kansas City, Missouri.
Photo courtesy Steve Loftin

1990 Ford station wagon provided for the Assistant Chief of the Tulsa Fire Dept., Tulsa, Oklahoma.
Photo courtesy Steve Loftin

1991 GMC Suburban, FDNY Battalion 41 Chief with an engine assignment in New York City.
Photo Courtesy John M. Calderone

1992 Chevrolet Caprice, driven by the Deputy Chief, Detroit Fire Dept., Detroit, Michigan. Photo courtesy Daniel Jasina

1995 Ford Crown Victoria provided for District 3 Chief of the Cincinnati Fire Dept., Cincinnati, Ohio. Photo courtesy Steve Hagy

1995 Chevrolet Caprice used by a Division Chief of FDNY. Rescue 5 is also on the scene in New York City. Photo courtesy John M. Calderone

The Kennedy Space Center Fire Rescue Logo.

1998 Ford Expedition in front of the NASA Spacecraft Assembly Building. Cape Canaveral Air Station and Kennedy Space Center Fire Departments combined to form two divisions under one command. This department protects our nation's space center in Florida, and is on alert at every space launch. The Incident Command wagon was modified to this configuration by Odyssey of Wharton, New Jersey.

Removable compartment unit installed.

The Odyssey control console from the driver's side.

Rear paint design and amber warning light bar.

Collectibles: fire chief vehicle toys and models

1960 Lincoln F.D. Chief, battery operated, "bump & go" tin toy car. Flashing top light and realistic siren noise. Manufactured by Yonezawa Toys LTD, Japan. Original cost: $1.45. 1998 flea market cost: $95.00.

1948 Chrysler sedan scale model. From the collection of Scott Schimpf.

1964 Ford hardtop plastic toy, manufactured for Grants 5&10 cents stores. Original cost: 39 cents. 1998 flea market cost: $12.00.

Chevrolet panel truck scale model. From the collection of Scott Schimpf.

1957 Chevrolet hardtop scale model. From the collection of Scott Schimpf.

1936 Ford coupe 1/43-scale model. Manufactured by The 43rd Ave. Collection of England. Very fine detail with Chicago markings, but black top is omitted.

Chief Carl Bechtold and his 1942 Chevrolet, purchased about 1945. This car was wrecked in 1948, on wet roads, going to a fire. It was replaced by a 1948 Chevrolet. Photo courtesy Bill Elliott

A 1946 Dodge DeLuxe sedan purchased by the Newark, New Jersey Fire Department for its 5th Battalion Chief. A new checkerboard grille replaced the prewar-style grille and would be used on all models until 1949. The 360-degree rotary beacon was made by Federal as a Model 17. This type of light would appear on police and fire vehicles for many years. Only fire cars used bells as a warning device. Note the rope passing through the body under the windshield.

Two 1946 Fords delivered to the Philadelphia, Pennsylvania Bureau of Fire. Cost $1,136 each. The immediate post-war models were virtually the same as the prewar models. The two-door sedans were equipped with the traditional locomotive bell up front and a Model ED-1 siren made by Sireno. Photos courtesy William Witt collection

This Battalion Chief's 1946 Ford is parked at a fire scene in St. Louis, Missouri. A B&M siren and Mars light share the front fenders. The two truck clearance lights on the roof light the front while two installed on the back belt line guard the rear. Photo courtesy Glenn Banz collection

The Toledo, Ohio Fire Department Deputy Chief's 1946 Pontiac Streamliner. This was the first Pontiac for Toledo after the war, and carried a price tag of $1,538 with $30 extra for the eight-cylinder engine. The roof-mounted red warning lights and Sterling siren stand out against the background. Photo courtesy Toledo Firefighters Museum

The Chief Engineer of Philadelphia, Pennsylvania, had this 1947 Buick sedan as his transportation. This "plain" car had small lettering on the door, but carried a beautiful chrome bell and a Mars light. Mars lights got peoples' attention by rotating about 90 degrees sideways. Photo courtesy Scott Schimpf

The 1947 Buick sedan was popular with a lot of fire companies. This is the Bureau of Fire, Chief of Wilkes-Barre, Pennsylvania, and his driver. The Roadmaster has a combination siren and light assembly. Some of these lights were designed to flash while others oscillated in the housing. Both attracted attention! Photo courtesy Jack Robrecht collection

Twin 1947 Chevrolet coupes purchased by the Bureau of Fire in Harrisburg, Pennsylvania. Both are marked Asst. Chief, but it's not hard to tell them apart. The car at left has a Sterling Model 20 siren with flasher light, while the one at right has a Federal Model EP siren. Both carry a warning light on the roof. Photo courtesy David Houseal collection

The Bureau of Fire in Reading, Pennsylvania, had this 1947 Chrysler New Yorker coupe for its Chief of the Department. Not many Chief cars have two sirens, as well as a locomotive bell. The siren on the left fender is a unique dual tone unit with tremendous volume of high- and low-pitch tones. With the other siren in concert, traffic would clear like magic. The white wheel trim rings may look out of place on a Fire Chief car, but were standard on all Chryslers due to whitewall tires not being available until April of 1947. Photo courtesy Jack Robrecht collection

This 1947 Nash Ambassador served the Racine, Wisconsin Fire Department. Nashes were built in Kenosha, just a few miles south of Racine. The paint job included neat gold leaf striping on this fastback sedan. The ED-1 siren and Mars light led the way. Photo courtesy Racine Firebell Museum Association

The New Haven, Connecticut Fire Department Chief's car was a 1947 Nash Ambassador Brougham club coupe. New Haven apparatus and cars are painted white. This 112-horsepower six-cylinder car cost $1,751. A Nash Ambassador was also the Official Pace Car for the 1947 Indianapolis 500. Photo courtesy Marvin Cohen

Harrisburg, Pennsylvania Fire Chief Earl Swartz used this 1948 Chrysler sedan in the performance of his duties. The radio-equipped car had a siren flasher light, roof-mounted warning light, and dual fog lights. Cost $2,041. Photo courtesy David Houseal collection.

The Fire Chief of St. Louis, Missouri, also used a 1948 Chrysler sedan until 1954. This "blue" car is equipped with a B&M siren and Mars light. Note the truck clearance lights on the front roof and the rear belt line. Photo courtesy Glenn Banz collection

A 1948 Dodge business coupe was used by the Asst. Chief of Lancaster, Pennsylvania. This radio-equipped, three-passenger car had a Federal dual tone siren light on the roof and dual warning lights on the front fenders. By 1948, the Dodge L-head six-cylinder engine was rated at 102 horsepower. Cost $1,587. Photo courtesy Bill Garrison

This 1948 Dodge business coupe was used by the Deputy Chief of Paterson, New Jersey. The siren is an early Model 66L Federal and is mounted on a custom L-shaped chrome pole attached to the bumper bracket through the splash pan. The bell is mounted in the same fashion. Photo courtesy Richard Adelman

A 1948 Packard sedan from the Boston, Massachusetts Fire Department. This radio-equipped Chief's car also has a Sireno R-2 siren and locomotive bell up front. A small 360-degree light on the roof may be the start of the Green Command signal light. The Fire Commissioner also drove a 1948 Packard Super Eight sedan. Cost $2,150. Photo courtesy Bob Noonan

The St. Louis Public Safety Director used a 1948 Packard limousine. This seven-passenger car with a 141-inch wheelbase weighed 4,880 pounds and cost the taxpayers $4,868. The Super eight-cylinder engine was rated at 145 horsepower. No siren showing, but a Mars light is mounted on the left front fender and the "St. Louis" truck clearance light is visible on the roof and above the rear bumper. Photo courtesy Glenn Banz collection

Canada's Vancouver Fire Department opened a new firehall in 1955, and rolled out this 1948 Plymouth club coupe for pictures. District Chief H. Foulkes and driver G. Temperton show off the car. A Sterling Model 30 Sirenlite is mounted on the fender. Note the pair of "football" warning lights mounted at 45 degrees on the roof! Photo courtesy of Alex Matches

In 1949, Ford produced a totally new automobile, new chassis, new body, and sold over 550,000 two-door, six-passenger sedans. Philadelphia Bureau of Fire, Chief of the Marine Division, used this unit with a front bell mount and roof light. Photo courtesy Scott Schimpf

This 1949 Buick Super sedan is ready for export to Bogota, Colombia. It is equipped with a roof-mounted Sterling Model 20 Sirenlite and dual fog and spotlights. Door lettering indicates its new owner was Station No. 1 Chief. Photo courtesy Bill Snyder

This decade of photos opened with the Naval Powder Factory Fire Department and closes with the same department. The Chief's car is now a 1949 Ford pickup truck with bubble light and small fender siren. Photo courtesy William Killen

NIFTY FIFTIES: 1950-1959

Looking back, upon entering into the second half of the 20th century, the tremendous progress automobiles had made can clearly be seen. What became everyday transportation for many of us was, in this case, a tool for the Chief of the fire department. As the favorite horse was led to pasture and the motorized vehicles took over, every day, sometimes every hour, a new use was found for the "Buggy."

As the hundreds of automobile manufacturers dwindled, and selection of brands narrowed, it was the user experience, and lower cost, that won the bid for staff automobiles. The cars were purchased on what was advertised in the bidding or available on a sales agreement (unlike the apparatus, which was built after the bidding was decided and took months to be delivered). Department Chiefs had the general public to thank for driver reports and quality control. Lots of past experience with a certain automobile manufacturer guided their decisions on bidding and purchasing.

At the mid-point of the 20th century, it may appear that the automobile had reached the pinnacle of its development and could not be improved much more. Events of the next fifty years guided automobile manufacture into new areas of style and design to increase both performance and economy to heights never before achieved. The fire service benefited from these improvements, but the result of greater operating safety was utmost in the minds of the staff leadership.

In this decade, these improvements included: larger trunk space; 12-volt, higher-ampere electrical systems for more electrical equipment; station wagon bodies for more utility; more powerful engines; tubeless tires; uniform controls; dual headlights; and seat belts.

The Battalion Chief's 1950 Ford sedan, in Paterson, New Jersey. This modern design car is framed by the older open cab tractor apparatus. A roof-mounted siren flasher combination unit, the front-mount bell, and installed radios are the department attachments. Photo courtesy Richard Adelman

An overhead shot of Battalion No. 6 of the Washington, D.C. Fire Department. The Battalion Chief and men of Engine Co. 16 and Truck 3 enter the second half of the 20th century equipped with these fire fighting machines: two 1947 Seagrave pumpers, a 1948 Seagrave 100-foot aerial truck, and the Chief's car, a 1946 Buick (also shown at ground level). Photos courtesy the late Len Sasher collection

This 1950 Buick Special Deluxe two-door sedan is one of many Buick automobiles purchased by the Baltimore City Fire Department. The Chief of the Salvage Corps was assigned this unit. A roof-mounted siren with flasher is the warning device. The famous portholes on the hood and the "buck tooth" grille are trademarks of the 1950s Buick. Cost $1,803. Photo courtesy R.D. Jennings collection

The Deputy Chief of Manchester, New Hampshire, drove this 1951 Chevrolet sedan. This Styleline Deluxe model was maroon in color, with matching fender skirts. It was radio equipped and had a Mars light mounted on the front fender.

This 1951 Chevrolet sport coupe was the Chief's car serving the Cranford, New Jersey Fire Department. The Chevy has an early style 66L Federal siren on the roof above the two-piece windshield. Cost $1,545. Photo courtesy John Schmidt

Battalion Chief 24 of the Baltimore City Fire Department was assigned this 1951 Buick Special. The roof-mounted siren is a Sterling Model 20. Note the one-piece windshield, and the amount of chrome trim as part of the design. Photo courtesy Bill Snyder

Battalion Chief 6 of the St. Louis, Missouri Fire Department drove a 1951 Ford. The front fenders carry a Mars Model GS siren made by B&M and a Mars light. The four corner clearance lights are on all fire department cars in the city. Photo courtesy Glenn Banz collection

One of the most unusual Asst. Chief vehicles was this 1951 Mack Model A squad car. Allentown, Pennsylvania, is home for the Mack truck factory, but this is taking local loyalty a bit too far. Photo courtesy Dan Martin/Jack Robrecht.

This picture was taken at a parade in Philadelphia. The Fire Chief, George Hink, is riding in the 1952 Buick Roadmaster sedan. A custom mounted bell and Federal "Q" siren are out front, and a Mars DX-40 light assembly is on the roof. Chief Hink and this Buick are also featured on the front cover of this book. A "Roto-Ray" was added to the front in the cover photograph. The second car in line is a 1953 Mercury Custom sedan with the Asst. Chief. It's equipped with a bell, Federal 78 dual tone siren and Federal Model 17 roof-mount bubble light. Photo courtesy Scott Schimpf

The Gary, Indiana Fire Department Asst. Chief was assigned this 1952 Ford two-door Ranch Wagon. This was a completely new body style for Ford Motor Co. The station wagon line would open new avenues for use by the fire service. This "Red Car" carried E&J inhalators, a folding stretcher, Geiger counter, and American Red Cross-approved first aid kits. Photo courtesy Wayne Stuart

This new 1952 Nash Statesman Chief's car was being checked out. The New Haven Fire Department in Connecticut paints all of its vehicles white. 1952 was the 50th anniversary of Nash Motor Co. Photo courtesy Marvin Cohen

Three 1953 Chevrolets of the Baltimore City Fire Department.

Battalion 7 Chief's Chevrolet with roof beacon and siren hidden behind the grille.

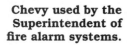

Chevy used by the Superintendent of fire alarm systems.

Same model Chevy was used by the Chief of the fire school. All three cars have 108-horsepower six-cylinder engines. The windshield is now one-piece without the center strip. Cost $1,620. Many large fire departments have fleets of same-brand automobiles. Photos courtesy Bill Snyder

Hyattsville, Maryland, Chief and his 1953 Ford Mainline two-door sedan. It was radio equipped and has a roof-mounted beacon. Photo courtesy Wayne Kidd collection

A 1953 Pontiac Chief's car serving St. Louis, Missouri. It's a Chieftain Deluxe model featuring the one-piece windshield and a wraparound rear window. It also featured ignition key starting for the first time in a Pontiac. Fire department attachments include a Mars light and a siren. Note the Mack truck (background) has a bell mounted in front of the grille. Photo courtesy Glenn Banz collection

This 1954 Cadillac was used by the Mayor of Hoboken, New Jersey, and then given to the fire department Chief after it was painted red. A perfect example of the old hand-me-down method of procurement. Photo courtesy Ron Schierle

A 1954 Pontiac sedan Chief's car serving St. Louis, Missouri. The fire department mounted a B&M siren and Mars light on the fenders. The maltese plate on the front bumper has a cross trumpet insignia in the center. Four corner clearance lights are mounted on the roof. Photo courtesy Glenn Banz collection

A V-8-powered 1955 Ford Ranch Wagon used by the Battalion 7 Chief in St. Louis, Missouri. The attached B&M siren and Mars light were standard for this fire department, as were the corner lights on the roof. Photo courtesy Glenn Banz collection

The Chief Training Instructor, Washington, D.C., used this 1955 Ford Customline sedan. A Federal WY siren with an oscillating Sola-Ray light was installed on the roof. Note Shelter Area sign on the firehouse. Photo courtesy Frank Tremel

A 1955 Ford Ranch Wagon, also V-8 powered, at a fire scene with a 1948 American LaFrance Model 700 pumper featuring matching two-tone paint. The Asst. Chief's car and the pumper were from the Muskegon, Michigan Fire Department. Photo courtesy Thomas Engle

A pair of Chiefs from Gary, Indiana, pose with a 1955 Ford Country Sedan station wagon. This was Ford's answer to a "Deluxe Wagon." Note the Studebaker-Packard dealership in the background. Photo courtesy Wayne Stuart

This 1955 Pontiac Star Chief sedan was top-of-the-line with a 173-horsepower engine. The Director of Public Safety in St. Louis, Missouri, parked the car in front of city hall. A Mars light on the front fender and an identification plate in the front are the only visible signs of official use. Whitewall tires and a sun shade are a few of the Pontiac's accessories. Cost $2,455. Photo courtesy Glenn Banz collection

A 1955 Pontiac Chieftain used by the Asst. Chiefs of FDNY. Car 12 has fender warning lights as well as a rotary-beacon on the roof. The rocker locomotive bell on the front was protected by the lower bumper, which was moved out six to eight inches. Photo courtesy Bob Schierle

This 1956 Buick Roadmaster was assigned to the Chief of FDNY Fire Patrol. Front fender warning lights and the roof rotary beacon give warning, especially at night. The bell mounting looks like a snow plow frame! Factory price $3,503. Photo courtesy Bob Schierle

A 1956 Buick Special assigned as the Division No. 2 Commanders car for the Boston, Massachusetts Fire Department. A Federal WL Model siren and full-size bell are mounted up front. The Buick is also equipped with both high- and low-band radios. Photo courtesy Charles A. Seaboyer

Fire Chief Rudy Anderson posed with his driver in a 1956 Dodge Coronet sedan. This Racine, Wisconsin, car has a Mars light and Federal 66G siren up front. In profile, the amount of trunk space available for fire fighting equipment and tools is evident. Photo courtesy Racine Firebell Museum Association

This 1956 Dodge Coronet was ready to carry the honored members of the Peekskill, New York Fire Department on parade. Note the whitewall tires and the curb feelers. A Federal WLRG siren is mounted on the roof of this two-tone Chief's sedan. At this time, Chrysler was installing Hemi V-8 engines with ratings up to 260 horsepower, Powerflite automatic transmissions, and full-time power steering. Photo courtesy Steve Cloutier collection

These 1956 Fords were a popular buy for fire department use, both as Chief "Wagons" and utility vehicles.

Customline two-door sedan used by Cincinnati, Ohio, District No. 1 Chief. The Federal Model Y siren and light is roof mounted. Photo courtesy Ed Effron

FDNY Car 793, a Customline sedan, carried a Battalion Chief on his duties. Added accessories included a Federal 170 series beacon, two fender-mounted red lights, maltese plate, rocker-type bell, and Federal Model 28 siren. Photo courtesy Bob Schierle

Polo, Illinois Fire Department Country Sedan station wagon, with a roof-mounted spotlight and a Federal Model 17 beacon light. Under-the-hood sirens were being installed on cars equipped with roof beacons. Photo courtesy Walt Schryver

Newark, New Jersey Fire Department's 2nd Division Deputy Chief used a 1956 Oldsmobile 88 sedan. It has a fender siren and bell and a roof beacon. It was powered by a 230-horsepower V-8 and cost $2,226. Photo courtesy Bob Schierle

This 1957 Chevrolet is the District No. 2 Chief's car in Cincinnati, Ohio. The two-door sedan has a Federal Type Y siren light on the roof. Note the mud/snow tires on the rear! Tire companies were producing this knobby tread tire as the replacement for chains. The tires helped, but chains were rated higher on traction and braking on ice. Photo courtesy Ed Effron

This 1957 Ford Custom Chief's car served the Washington, D.C. Fire Department. It carried Plate No.3 and is equipped with a Federal Model 17 beacon and Model 28 siren cut into the grille. The 190-horsepower V-8 sedan cost $2,142. Late-1950s automobiles had a huge selection of engines and options.

"The Passing of the Keys" was symbolic on behalf of the fire department and the local car dealer. A dealer is shown handing over a key to Chief Tom Diese of the Sacramento, California Fire Department, on delivery of five 1957 Pontiacs. The dealers used photo opportunities such as this for promotional purposes in newspaper ads and write-ups. It also gave the fire department a record for its archives. The factory price on these Chieftain sedans was $2,527 each, equipped with a 290-horsepower V-8. (L-R) Captain Davis, Chief "Knobby" Diese, Chief Mangan, Chief Humphies, Chief Ripley, and Chief Tom Diese accepting the key from an unidentified dealer. Photo courtesy Pioneer Mutual Hook & Ladder Society

This 1957 Pontiac is a Training Division Deputy Chief's "Wagon" from Hartford, Connecticut Fire Department. The Super Chief station wagon was parked at a training site along with a B model Mack pumper (note the hose going up the steps into the building in the background). The Super Chief is equipped with a Federal roof beacon and spotlight, but is missing two of its three decorative "stars" off the rear quarter panel. Photo courtesy Scott Schimpf

This combination of fire fighters belong to the Rahway Fire Department in New Jersey. The 1957 Plymouth Savoy two-door sedan has a roof-mounted siren light to match the location of the siren on the American LaFrance Model 700 aerial truck. This was the first model Plymouth with dual headlights. Options included power brakes and power steering. Photo courtesy Bob Schierle

Chicago, Illinois Fire Department 22nd Battalion Chief's 1958 Chevrolet station wagon. A Mars DX-40 unit is mounted in the center of the roof between the green and red warning lights of Chicago fame. Dual Mars 888 lights are on the fenders. Chicago also continues the black over red two-tone painting. Photo courtesy Bob Schierle

Washington, D.C. Fire Department 4th Battalion Chief's 1958 Chevy station wagon. This Brookwood has the siren mounted in the grille, and a roof-mounted Federal beacon. Note the left door has no markings or trim. Replaced or repaired! Photo courtesy Len Sasher collection

Tulsa, Oklahoma Fire Department's Car 102 was a 1958 Chevy Delray sedan assigned to District No. 2 Chief. The car has a B&M siren and Federal beacon. It was reported that this was the last Chief's car to have a motor siren. Electronics is on the way! Photo courtesy Steve Loftin collection

The Chicago Fire Department also had 1958 Ford Battalion Chief cars. This Country Sedan station wagon was outfitted with the same lighting and warning system as the aforementioned 1958 Chevrolets. Photo courtesy Bob Schierle

This 1958 Mercury sedan is Chief car No. 1 from the Covington, Kentucky Fire Department. The 360-degree warning light on the roof is the only light visible. Note the beautiful stone facade of the fire station. Photo courtesy Ed Effron

An ultra-trim 1958 Oldsmobile 98 sedan serving the Atlantic City, New Jersey Fire Department. This Chief's car had its share of stainless trim and chrome plating. A roof-mounted siren tops the accessories of this 305-horsepower car. Factory price $3,824. The Olds weighed 4,474 pounds. Photo courtesy Bob Schierle

Plymouth built a large wagon in 1958. This was the 3rd Battalion Chief's Suburban in front of Engine 15 House in Washington D.C. The Suburban was built on a 122-inch wheelbase with an overall length of 213.1 inches. The siren is mounted under the left headlights with the motor in the grille. The roof beacon gave 360-degree coverage. Photo courtesy the late Len Sasher collection

The Albany, New York Fire Department purchased a 1959 Buick Invicta hardtop for duty. Battalion Chief Richard D. Fleming posed with the all-new style Buick equipped with a 325-horsepower 401-cubic inch V-8 engine. Factory price $3,447. A Mars Model DX-40 roof light and a Federal 66G siren were added. Note the neat combination spotlight/mirror. Photo courtesy Mark Boock

This 1959 Ford Battalion Chief's car attracted a lot of attention in St. Louis, Missouri. This Country Sedan station wagon has a Federal 17 rotary beacon on the roof while a B&M siren is sticking through the center of the grille. Photo courtesy Glenn Banz collection

Profile view of a 1959 Ford Tudor, from Vancouver, B.C., equipped with a Federal "Q" siren on the roof. The Asst. Chief on duty used this car for fire calls. Note the slight trim difference on this Canadian Ford compared to its U.S. counterpart. Photo courtesy Alex Matches

Three Chiefs from Rome, New York, tried to hide their "armored water guns," but they weren't quite tall enough! They did hide the better part of their 1959 Plymouth Savoy sedan. Photo courtesy William Cary

This 1959 Plymouth Suburban was the Asst. Chief's car serving Muskegon, Michigan. It has a rotary beacon and a Mars 888 light and small siren on the roof. Photo courtesy Thomas Engle

This 1959 Mercury Montclair sedan was No. 1 in the St. Louis, Missouri Fire Department. Fire Chief James Muller used this black car (still using a forward-hinged hood) from 1959-1966. Cost $3,308. Photo courtesy Glenn Banz collection

The FDNY Chief used this black 1959 Mercury in the performance of his duties. The maltese plate is "Number One"! Note the custom-install double pair of warning lights above the bumper. Photo courtesy the Mand Library & Research Center of New York

The FDNY has simultaneous operations in a six-story warehouse and thirteen old law tenements in Harlem. This "spectacular" multi-alarm fire required several battalions of manpower including the Chiefs. The early-1950s Chevrolet sedans (lower left) are the Chief "Wagons."

SLICK SIXTIES: 1960-1969

The Chief "Wagons" begin this decade with jet aircraft-inspired body designs and more horsepower under the hood. Viewing the yearly changes in the bodies and grilles, the aircraft styling influence slowly fades to a smooth-sided, stainless trim-adorned exterior. Aluminum grilles and trim become fashionable, and dual headlights are standard. Station wagons remained popular with fire departments.

Engines are the focus of attention in the 1960s. Police cars lead the pursuit for bigger engines with more horsepower. Dodge produced a 440 cubic inch V-8 to chase the Lincolns with 462 cubic inch V-8s and Cadillacs with 500 cubic inch V-8s. The horsepower race continued into the early-1970s, and many of the Fire Chief cars were purchased with police packages of higher horsepower output.

The 360-degree beacon grew in popularity to a point of necessity. The aircraft warning system lent itself to emergency vehicles so well that the industry adopted it nearly 100 percent. The motorist sharing the roadway with fire and police departments saw the new beacons as the authority on the road, and heeded its rotating beams. The light beams moving in a circular pattern gave advance warning in all directions.

Previously optional equipment became standard, such as seat belts, telescoping steering columns, windshield washers, backup lights, and dual master brake cylinders. The shift lever was moved to the steering column, and Chrysler started the use of the alternator for low-speed charging. It replaced the generator, a standard accessory on engines for 45 years. DeSoto production was dropped by Chrysler, and the International Scout appeared on the scene with "4WD." Four-wheel-drive-equipped vehicles became part of the American automotive landscape and improved the fire department's ability to get going in all kinds of weather.

Evident while viewing these photos of the 1960s, the polished bells are gone from Chief cars, but the "bubble gum machines" are now the rage.

To open the 1960s decade, this photograph shows a Philadelphia Fire Department Truck Co. on the scene of a four alarm fire. It was located in the powerhouse that supplied power to the Reading train system. A master stream is being pumped into the fire while the wind is driving the heavy smoke over the railroad. Twenty thousand people were stranded in center city due to the train service interruption. The Chief arrived on the scene with his driver in this new 1960 Pontiac four-door sedan. Photo courtesy Michael Hink collection

Chief "Buck" Steadman was ready to step into his 1960 Dodge Dart station wagon. The Winona Fire Department is located in Minnesota. This Pioneer could be bought with an engine as small as a 145-horsepower six up to a 383-cubic inch V-8 rated at 325 horsepower for $2,906. Whitewall tires were $33 extra. Photo courtesy Michael Rybarczyk

This 1960 Ford Ranch Wagon was assigned to the Battalion 10 Chief stationed at Engine Co. 14 house, in Baltimore, Maryland. The roof-mounted siren is a Sireno Model R-5-R. Photo courtesy Bill Snyder

A 1960 Plymouth Suburban assigned to the Deputy Chief (the car carries plate No. 2) of the Washington, D.C. Fire Department. The horsepower race was "hotter than fresh pancakes." Plymouth was installing engines in its cars that produced 310 horsepower from 361 cubic inches. The company called this engine "Golden Commando." Photo courtesy the late Len Sasher collection

Passaic, New Jersey, Chief of the Fire Auxiliary drove this 1961 Chevrolet well into the 1980s when this photograph was taken. The car was showing its age with rust evident around the rear wheel well. This Brookwood model was one of 169,000 station wagons built in 1961. Photo courtesy Ernest Rodrigues

This FDNY Battalion Chief's car was a 1961 Dodge Dart Seneca station wagon. Car 879 is shown with Ladder 196 with the 700 series ALF open cab tractor. The 1961 Dodge bodyside and taillight design was part of the jet era styling. The tailgate had a crankdown window and opened down to extend the floor space. Photo courtesy Bob Schierle

The 1961 Ford Ranch Wagon was parked in front of the Washington, D.C. Fire Department Training Center. The three admirers checking out the Chief's car are the three brothers: See No, Speak No, and Hear No. Photo courtesy the late Len Sasher collection

This Chief's car from Clifton, New Jersey, is a 1961 Mercury Monterey sedan. Car 81 is shown at a fire scene amidst charged lines. Photo courtesy Ernest Rodrigues

This 1961 Oldsmobile 98 is parked near the clean-up and investigation scene of a structure fire in Toledo, Ohio. The Town Sedan has a roof beacon, Mars 888 light and Mars siren. This stylish beauty was equipped with double line whitewalls. Photo courtesy Toledo Firefighters Museum

Chief Robert M. Houseal (left) accepts the keys for this 1961 Pontiac Catalina sedan from the salesman, while driver William Wertz looks on. This "Key Ceremony" in Harrisburg, Pennsylvania, is a typical event when the Chief gets a new "Buggy." A new Federal 66G siren was installed. Photo courtesy David Houseal

This 1961 Rambler Classic station wagon was the Chief's car for the fire department in the town of Los Gatos in Santa Clara County, California. The town had a small, paid department until 1971, when the county took over. This happens to Fire Chiefs all over the country. It's called "consolidation." Two 360-degree flashers are mounted on the roof. Note the town seal on the door and the factory optional roof rack. Photo courtesy Don Jarvis

Two views of a 1962 Dodge FDNY Battalion Chief's car 917. This Dart series station wagon is equipped with Federal beacon, red fender lights, matching painted siren, and bumper-mounted bell. Photos courtesy Bob Schierle

A 1962 Ford Ranch Wagon used by the 2nd Battalion Chief in Washington, D.C. Note the four-bulb rotary beacon has a clear lens. Photo courtesy Scott Schimpf

A 1962 Ford Galaxie sedan assigned to the Deputy Chief of the Lexington Fire Department in Massachusetts. It has a combination spotlight/mirror. The band antenna and beacon are mounted on the roof. Photo courtesy Scott Schimpf

This 1962 Pontiac Star Chief sedan was the Chief's car serving the Memphis, Tennessee Fire Department. Factory price $3,097. A Federal C-6 siren light and two spotlights are attached. Is that Graceland under construction across the street? Photo courtesy Steve Loftin collection

This V-8-powered 1962 Rambler Ambassador was parked in front of Station 5 in Racine, Wisconsin. A Federal "Q" siren and Mars light are first class accessories. The car was destroyed in 1967, when responding to a call. The Asst. Chief was injured in the accident. Photo courtesy Racine Firebell Museum Association

North Plainfield, New Jersey, had white fire rigs, and this 1963 Chevrolet Chief's car was no exception. It is a Biscayne station wagon. Cost $2,723. The rig peeking out of the station is a Mack. Photo courtesy Bob Schierle

Back to Memphis, Tennessee, and this 1963 Ford 300 sedan Deputy Chief's car with a Federal C-6 siren and light. Dual spotlights are also added equipment. Photo courtesy Steve Loftin collection

The military posts of our armed forces have their own fire departments. At Fort Dix, New Jersey, the Fire Chief used this radio-equipped 1963 Ford pickup truck as his Chief's unit. Photo courtesy Bob Schierle

A 1963 Pontiac Catalina sedan used by the Deputy Chief in the City of Baltimore, Maryland. Fire Chief cars were using under-the-hood sirens. Both motor- and electronic-type were being installed. Photo courtesy Bill Snyder

This 1963 Rambler Ambassador 880 station wagon was assigned to the Chief of Westfield, New Jersey. Supersized red warning lights were mounted on the roof aside the beacon. Note the roof rack! Photo courtesy Bob Schierle

Car 63257 is a 1963 Studebaker Lark Regal metallic brown color two-door sedan assigned to Battalion No. 6 Chief of Philadelphia, Pennsylvania. Cost $2,055. Note the loudspeaker mounted on the roof. Photo courtesy Bob Schierle

A 1964 Buick Wildcat sedan equipped with a Federal 66G siren and a roof beacon. This Harrisburg, Pennsylvania, Chief's car was parked on the riverfront walkway along the Susquehanna River. The fire fighters on this shift were pressure checking hose. Wildcat price $3,164. Photo courtesy Ron Helman

A 1964 Chevrolet Biscayne station wagon used by the Battalion No. 3 Chief at a New Jersey fire scene along with apparatus of the Jersey City Fire Department. Photo courtesy Ron Jeffers

A 1964 Ford Country Sedan station wagon assigned to the 1st District Chief of Louisville, Kentucky. The Federal "Q" siren on the fender and the roof beacon cleared the traffic. Cost of the Ford was $3,000 with a standard V-8 engine, but more in this case, as the car came equipped with the big-block 427-cubic inch engine as indicated by the fender badge behind the front wheel. Photo courtesy Steve Loftin collection

Chief of the 1st Battalion in Albany, New York, drove this 1965 Dodge Polara station wagon that weighed 4,220 pounds and cost $3,110. The double end light is a Mars DX-40. Speaker on the roof supports the siren system. Photo courtesy Steve Loftin collection

Protecting our troops overseas in Vietnam was the job of the Army Engineers Fire Chief. He was assigned this 1965 M151 jeep. This picture was taken at the Cu Chi Vietnam base camp of the 25th Infantry Division. The rotary beacon was removed from a destroyed UH-1 helicopter. No siren was installed because sirens were used to signal incoming mortar rounds. Photo courtesy William T. Wilcox

A 1965 Pontiac Star Chief sedan serving the Norwood, Massachusetts Fire Department. The Chief's car was radio equipped and has a beacon warning on the roof as well as an electronic speaker system. Pontiac offered four sizes of V-8 engines, up to 376 horsepower. Photo courtesy Scott Schimpf

Chief Hamilton of the Memphis, Tennessee Fire Department was provided with this 1965 Pontiac Bonneville hardtop sedan. It is equipped with a roof-mounted siren unit and two spotlight/mirrors. Factory price $3,362, without options. Photo courtesy John Schmidt

The Bureau of Fire in Scranton, Pennsylvania, assigned this 1966 Dodge Polara sedan to the Fire Chief. Cost $2,838. The rotary beacon base housed the siren speaker. The ornate cut stone building in the background is the city hall. Photo courtesy Mark Boock

The 2nd Battalion Chief of the Washington, D.C. Fire Department had this 1966 Ford Ranch Wagon washed and ready to go. A Federal C-5G siren is mounted on the front fender and a clear lens rotary beacon is on the roof. Note the poster in the rear window, which reads: "Help Us Put Them Out - D.C. Fire Department." Photo courtesy Scott Schimpf

The Deputy Chief's car, serving the Kearny, New Jersey Fire Department, at a fire scene. This 1967 Chevrolet Impala sedan was radio equipped and had a roof beacon. Note the boy in the background using his coat to cover his mouth due to heavy smoke in the air. Photo courtesy Ron Jeffers

The Fire Chief's 1967 Ford Custom sedan serving the Washington, D.C. Fire Department. A Federal C-5G siren is custom mounted on the fender and a 360-degree beacon is on the roof. Photo courtesy the late Len Sasher collection

A 1967 Ford Custom sedan assigned to the District Chief of the Memphis, Tennessee Fire Department. Memphis uses Federal C-6 sirens. The fender badge behind the front wheel identifies the power source as a big-block 428-cubic inch V-8. Photo courtesy Richard Adelman

Car 82 is a 1967 Mercury Commuter station wagon assigned to the Deputy Chief of the Clifton, New Jersey Fire Department. It's hard to keep the equipment clean with slushy roads so common in winter! Photo courtesy Ernest Rodrigues

A bright yellow 1968 Plymouth Fury sedan used by the Ann Arbor, Michigan Fire Department. This picture was taken after the car was repainted yellow (retaining its original white top). The department's 1st Battalion Chief's car was red for several years. Note the red lens-lower headlights and light bar with clamp-on rails. The light bar would be the state-of-the-art emergency warning system for many years. Photo courtesy Richard L. Story

Two 1968 Buick Wildcat Fire Chief cars from Harrisburg, Pennsylvania. The Chief parked in front of the Harrisburg Hospital and the Asst. Chief parked at the entrance to the State Capitol. These big V-8-powered cars were rated at 360 horsepower. Cost $3,416. Note the simulated air vents of the jet-inspired styling. Photo courtesy Ron Helman

This unusual Deputy Chief's car was assigned to 3rd Division of the Newark, New Jersey Fire Department. It's a 1968 Checker Marathon station wagon. Cost $3,491. Checkers were available with six- or eight-cylinder engines supplied by Chevrolet. The tilt of the bumper, missing trim and numerous dents are evidence the Checker endured hard duty by the time this picture was taken in 1977. Photo courtesy Ron Jeffers

A good example of why closed cars with heaters are better than the open roadsters of yesteryear. This FDNY Battalion Chief's 1968 Ford station wagon was in the garage to thaw out! Photo courtesy the Mand Library & Research Center of New York

A 1968 Pontiac Catalina sedan was the Fire Chief's car serving Asheville, North Carolina. It's shown at the fire scene with Engine No. 1, an American LaFrance 900 series pumper. Photo courtesy Jack Ramsey

This gold leaf-trimmed 1969 Ford Country Sedan station wagon was assigned to the Chief of the West Patterson, New Jersey Fire Department. This is a rare exception to find a Fire Chief car decorated with gold leaf, even in 1969. Note the "For Sale" sign in the window. Virginian Tommy Herman purchased the car. Photo courtesy Tommy Herman

This five alarm fire scene is at night, but the fire and surrounding apparatus lighting gave the photographer enough light to shoot this picture. The 1961 Studebaker "Lark" two-door sedan is the 3rd Battalion Chief's car. The night winds are fanning the flames of the Joseph Singerly school, located at 22nd and Berks St. in Philadelphia, Pennsylvania. The building was 72 years old and completely destroyed by the blaze. Photo courtesy Michael Hink

PINNACLE PERIOD: 1970-1979

The automobile reached its pinnacle as far as engine size and horsepower during the decade of the 1970s. Downsizing of both automobiles and engines would only begin after the public rebelled against big cars and their resulting poor gas mileage. Gasoline prices climbed after the oil embargo of 1973 and the crunch that followed, but neither affected the fire service beyond a few curtailments. Fuel economy also was not a concern to the fire service, but performance remained an important factor. The unleaded gas, along with the emissions standards passed by the government, would cause problems with new car selection and bidding. The fire department would continue to purchase full-size sedans and station wagons. Imports would gain in popularity, but could not enter the market for emergency vehicles because of their small size.

Four-wheel-drive vehicles were available from Chevrolet, GMC, Ford, American Motors and International, but were more truck than car. The fire companies in the mountain states purchased these workhorses for their Chiefs, but most city and town fire departments still believed in using chains and knobby tires in bad weather.

Some of the design improvements during this period included steel-belted radial tires, disc brakes, electronic ignition, and brighter quartz-halogen lights. The roof-mounted single emergency light beacon moved to a bar attachment and was mated with other electronic gear. The signal manufacturers quickly developed an emergency light bar that matched a dual rotary beacon setup. This type of emergency light would continue to improve and flash its way into the end of the century.

Robert J. Quinn was Fire Commissioner of Chicago when this black 1970 Cadillac Fleetwood was provided for him. Photo courtesy Hank Sajovic

This 1970 Dodge Polara was a Chief's car assigned to the Pittsburgh, Pennsylvania Bureau of Fire. These full-size sedans also saw much duty as police cars. Cost $3,222. Photo courtesy John Schmidt

This 1970 Mercury Monterey was typical of the size cars used during the early-1970s, before the gas crunch. The door marking indicates it was a Chief's car with the Clifton, New Jersey Fire Public Safety Department. Photo courtesy Ernest Rodrigues

This lime green 1970 Chevrolet station wagon was Car 101. The Chief of the Fire Auxiliary from Passaic, New Jersey, was assigned this unit. By the end of the 1970s, light bars such as this mount would capture its share of the emergency light market. Photo courtesy Ernest Rodrigues

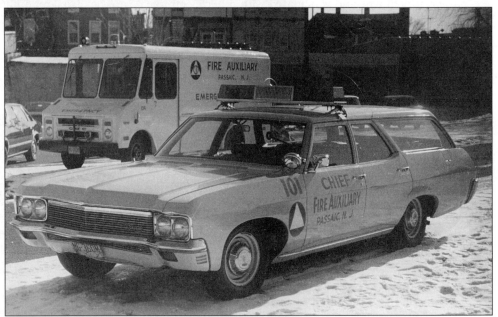

Jamestown, New York Fire Department provided this 1971 Ford Ranch Wagon for its Chief. Dual spotlights and roof beacon are visible on this radio-equipped car. Station wagons were popular with officials because they had ample cargo space. Photo courtesy Leo Duliba

A full-size 1971 Plymouth Fury I sedan was provided for the 9th Battalion Chief of the San Francisco, California Fire Department. Dual red lights and a beacon were installed on the roof. Photo courtesy Bill Egan

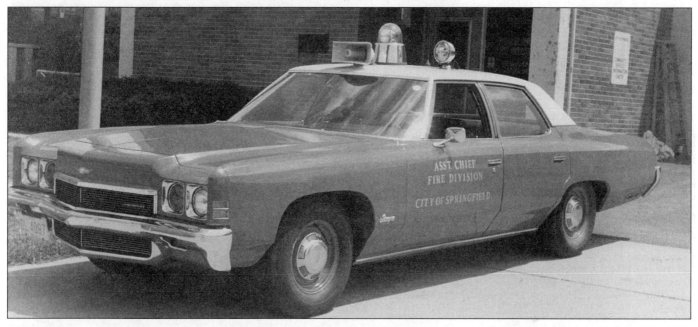

This full-size 1972 Chevrolet Biscayne sedan was the Asst. Chief's ride in Springfield, Ohio. The car weighed 4,045 pounds and cost $3,408. Note the high beam headlights are converted to warning lights in addition to the roof equipment. Photo courtesy Roger Bjorge

A 1972 Mercury Monterey station wagon was provided for the Deputy Chief from the Clifton, New Jersey Fire Department. It was Car 82. Photo courtesy Ernest Rodrigues

The Fire Chief of the City of Baltimore, Maryland Fire Department used this "Black Beauty!" This 1972 Pontiac Grand Ville hardtop sedan had a detachable light bar over its vinyl roof. Base price $4,507. Photo courtesy Scott Schimpf

A 1973 Chevrolet Bel Air station wagon was assigned to the Asst. Chief of the Kearny, New Jersey Fire Department. A Sireno action bar is mounted on the roof and has a Model 199 Sky-lighter and two Model MC2 Saf-T-Ray flashing lights. A Sireno motor siren was also mounted under the hood. Photo courtesy Craig Stewart

Note the light bar and whitewall tires on this 1973 Chevrolet Bel Air sedan. Car 91 was the call sign for this Passaic, New Jersey, Chief's car. Photo courtesy Ernest Rodrigues

Safety yellow was the color of this 1973 Chrysler Newport sedan from Evergreen Park, Illinois Fire Department. The high beam headlights have red lenses to supplement the two large beacons and warning lights on the roof bar. Factory price $4,693 without options. Photo courtesy Roger Bjorge

Mount Lebanon Township, Pennsylvania Fire Department provided this yellow 1973 AMC Matador sedan for its Fire Chief. American Motors sold a lot of this model for police fleets. Cost $2,853 without options. Photo courtesy John Schmidt

The "Big Four" automakers of 1974 produced "five-door" station wagons to attract the buying public, who desired space and utility. The fire service put the wagons to good use employing their large cargo areas, convertible seating, and ample horsepower. The following four cars pictured are comparable models for 1974.

AMC Matador Chief's wagon from the Harrisburg, Pennsylvania Bureau of Fire. AMC sold over 16,500 full-size station wagons. Average cost $4,200 less options. Photo courtesy James Derstine

Plymouth Suburban Chief's wagon from the St. Louis, Missouri Fire Department. Plymouth sold over 19,500 full-size wagons. Average cost $4,900 less options. Photo courtesy Steve Loftin collection

Chevrolet Bel Air Chief's wagon from the Parsons, Kansas Fire Department. Chevrolet sold over 35,000 full-size wagons. Average cost $4,700 less options. Photo courtesy Steve Loftin collection

Ford Country Sedan Chief's wagon from the Anadarko, Oklahoma Fire Department. Ford sold over 98,500 full-size wagons. Average cost $4,650 less options. Photo courtesy Steve Loftin collection

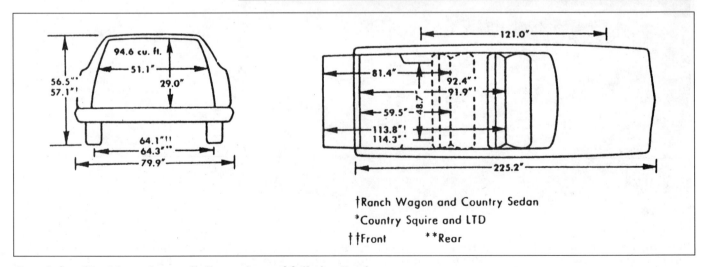

†Ranch Wagon and Country Sedan

*Country Squire and LTD

††Front   **Rear

Drawings of inside and overall dimensions of full-size Fords.

This 1975 AMC Matador station wagon is a Battalion Chief's car from Rochester, New York. 1975 was the first year of electronic ignition and unleaded gasoline use. Engines were de-rated 30 to 50 horsepower (an average of 22 percent) due to government-enforced emissions controls on engines. Photo courtesy Roger Bjorge

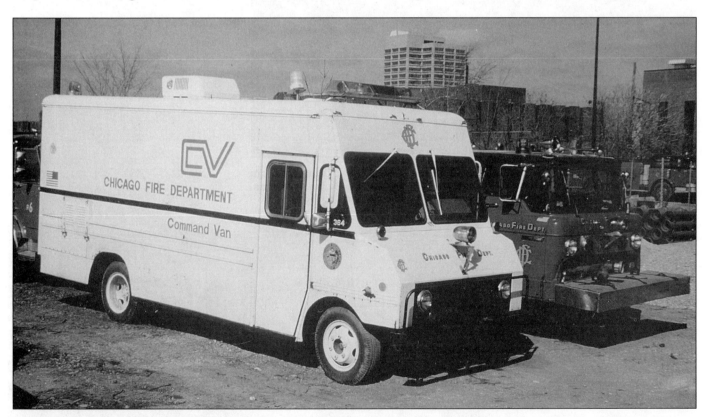

Changes in staff vehicle make-up were occurring, which, in turn, affected the Chief and his Chief Officers. Shown is a converted 1975 Ford van assigned to the Chicago Fire Department. The Command Post moved from the back of station wagons to vans such as this, for major disasters. This "office" had large generators and electrical equipment to provide the Chief and his subordinates a control center linking all communications. Maps and charts would later give way to computers and data files. Photo courtesy Hank Sajovic

The U.S. Army in Korea had American Civil Service Fire Chiefs and used American vehicles for Chief "Wagons."

Chief James Derstine was assigned to part of the DMZ in Paju County using this 1975 Dodge pickup. The Dodge had the normal red lights, beacon, and electronic siren, but also had a half-inch steel floor under the cab to protect Derstine from field mines. The extra weight made the truck ride like a tank. He kept his gear and tools in the box in the bed. The box was hand-made with a wooden logo.

The Asst. Chief used this CJ5 Jeep within the western corridor and Paju County, covering 355 square miles, and 127 towns with 5 fire stations. Photos courtesy James Derstine

Two C5J Jeeps at Camp Grant, Korea. The Fire Marshal and the Asst. Fire Marshal used these Chief's vehicles along the western corridor of the DMZ.

The Air Force Fire Chief at Plattsburg AFB in New York was provided with this 1976 Chevrolet Suburban half-ton truck. Chevrolet would retain the Suburban name for the rest of the century. Photo courtesy James Derstine

This late-1977 Buick LeSabre sedan saw duty in Milwaukee, Wisconsin. The Deputy Chief parked his car in front of a round-fender Peter Pirsch pumper. Buick was manufacturing a V-6 engine for use in cars of this size. Note the double speaker light bar. Photo courtesy Roger Bjorge

This white over red painted 1977 Ford LTD station wagon had a C-1 plate symbolizing the Chief of the Monroe, Michigan Fire Department. This LTD wagon weighed 4,635 pounds and cost $5,415 less options. Photo courtesy R.D. Jennings

A 1977 Ford LTDII 'S' sedan from Montreal, Quebec, Canada. Car 107 was used by the shift commander. That's French lettering on the door. Photo courtesy James Derstine

A 1977 Plymouth Volare sedan provided for the Battalion Chiefs of the Pittsburgh, Pennsylvania Fire Department. Pittsburgh Chiefs used this size of vehicle from 1977 to 1981. Photo courtesy John Schmidt

This unmarked 1978 Ford Granada sedan was a Chief's car that saw duty with the Cushing, Oklahoma Fire Department. The roof bar is a Federal Streethawk, with red and blue lenses. Photo courtesy Steve Loftin collection

A 1978 Chevrolet Impala sedan assigned to the Asst. Chief from Harrisburg, Pennsylvania. Photo courtesy David Houseal collection

The Deputy Chief from the Hoboken, New Jersey Fire Department used a 1978 Chevrolet Series 30 Sport Van equipped with a Federal Twinsonic roof bar. This full-size van was popular for emergency service use. Cost $6,439 and up. Photo courtesy Ron Jeffers

The Deputy Chief's 1978 Dodge Monaco station wagon at a fire scene in Clifton, New Jersey. Photo courtesy Ernest Rodrigues

A full-size 1979 Chevrolet Impala sedan serving the Ft. Smith, Arkansas Fire Department. Car 50 was the Chief's radio call. A Federal Twinsonic roof bar is mounted up top. Note the thin line whitewall tires. Photo courtesy Steve Loftin collection

This full-size Ford LTDII saw duty with the Holdenville, Oklahoma Fire Department. The Chief's car is typical of the 1977-79 Ford sedans used by the fire service. A Federal Twinsonic light bar and twin spotlights are the visible accessories. Photo courtesy Steve Loftin collection

SEDANS TO SUBURBANS: 1980-1989

The 1980s period of fire department automotive history contains the acceptance and growing use of four-wheel-drive vehicles and the larger cargo-carrying utility vans. The carmakers continued to produce full-size sedans and station wagons, extending the series run of some body styles by more than 10 years. Compact cars and front-wheel-drive gained favor with the public during this period, but the fire service continued to buy full-size rear-wheel-drive vehicles. Police departments continued to purchase full-size cars equipped with police packages, but without four-wheel-drive conversion. The high degree of quality found in import cars forced American engineers to "raise the bar" in their automotive design.

Sedans were still prevalent in metro city fire operations for staff officers, with use of station wagons slowly disappearing at the battalion level. New purchase upgrades replaced the wagons with 4x4 Blazers, Broncos, and Wagoneers. Metro areas started using the biggest Chevrolet and GMC Suburbans. The emergency vehicles were perceived to be heavy-duty, do-everything, haul-all, must-go-anywhere-type vehicles. The emergency light bar continued to top the roofs of all emergency vehicles.

The "Big Four" domestic manufacturers were reduced to the "Big Three" with the buyout of American Motors by Chrysler in the late-1980s. The Jeep name was an important part of the purchase, and its four-wheel-drive business would boost Chrysler sales. The fire service purchased its share of Jeeps.

Fire Chief vehicles in this section are grouped by manufacturer.

> The Dodge Diplomat sedan production run began in 1977 and continued with the same basic body until 1989. These four Fire Chief cars were selected to represent the Diplomats in use during this period. All eight-cylinder cars had a 318 cubic inch engine and cost $5,647 in 1979 and $12,010 to $14,795 in 1989.

Battalion 41 Chief from Anne Arundel County Fire Department, Maryland.

Chief Car 13 from Riviera Beach Volunteer Fire Company, Maryland.

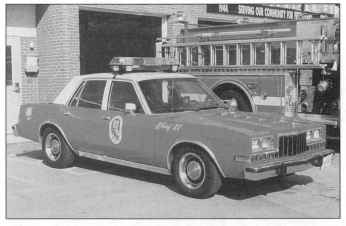

Chief Car 27 from Morningside Volunteer Fire Department, Maryland.

Chief Car 40 from West Annapolis Volunteer Fire Department, Maryland. Photos courtesy John D. Floyd, Jr.

General Motors' full-size entry for the fire service during the 1980s was the Chevrolet Caprice. This model was launched in 1966 and continued as a full-size sedan and station wagon until 1996. The following Caprice Fire Chief cars illustrate a variety of paint schemes as well as the individual choice of warning system installations.

A 1986 Caprice from Braddock Heights Volunteer Fire Department, Maryland. Car 12 is white with a red stripe. Photo courtesy John D. Floyd, Jr.

A 1988 Caprice from Tuckerton Fire Department, New Jersey. It's white over red with a white stripe. Photo courtesy Art Knobloch

A 1988 Caprice from Wheaton Fire Department, Illinois. The black over red paint emulates the Chicago design. Photo courtesy Ron Bogardus

A 1989 Caprice from Roseland Fire Department, New Jersey. It's white with multiple red stripes. Photo courtesy Art Knobloch

Car 614 is a tomato red 1983 Caprice station wagon assigned to the District 4 Chief of the Tulsa Fire Department, Oklahoma. Photo courtesy Steve Loftin collection

Chief's car C-3 is a red 1986 Caprice station wagon from Caledonia Fire Department, Wisconsin. Photo courtesy Racine Firebell Museum Association

Car 701 is a white 1985 Caprice Classic station wagon from Broken Arrow Fire Department, Oklahoma. Cost $11,571. Photo courtesy Steve Loftin collection

This Battalion Chief's 1987 Caprice station wagon is from Port Huron Fire Department, Michigan. It's painted a soft yellow color with a reflecting stripe. Photo courtesy Daniel Jasina

The Ford Motor Co. also offered the public a full-size sedan and station wagon. The fire service used both versions of the Crown Victoria in the performance of its duties. The car is a favorite with many fire departments. The following are a sampling of the many 1980s "Crown Vics" on duty.

A black over red 1983 Battalion Chief's sedan from Chicago Fire Department, Illinois. Photo courtesy Hank Sajovic

A red 1985 Chief's sedan from Freehold Fire Department, New Jersey. Photo courtesy Arthur Knobloch

A maroon 1988 Deputy Chief's sedan from Philadelphia, Pennsylvania. Photo courtesy Andrew Witt

A fire engine red 1989 Chief's sedan from Edwardsville Fire Department, Kansas. Photo courtesy Steve Loftin collection

Car 37 is a white 1989 Chief's sedan from Weatherford Fire Department, Oklahoma. Photo courtesy Steve Loftin collection

This red 1982 station wagon served the Jenks Fire Department, Oklahoma. Photo courtesy Steve Loftin collection

A red 1982 Chief's wagon from Verdigris Fire District, in Oklahoma. Photo courtesy Steve Loftin collection

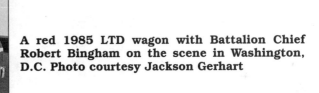

A red 1985 LTD wagon with Battalion Chief Robert Bingham on the scene in Washington, D.C. Photo courtesy Jackson Gerhart

A red 1989 Chief's wagon serving the Freehold Fire Department, New Jersey. Photo courtesy Arthur Knobloch

This bronze 1981 Pontiac LeMans Safari Battalion Chief's wagon saw duty with the Passaic, New Jersey Fire Department. Photo courtesy Ernest Rodriques

Fire Commissioner William Blair of Chicago, Illinois, was provided with this 1981 Oldsmobile 98 sedan. Full wheel covers and whitewall tires dress up this all black car. Photo courtesy Hank Sajovic

The 1982 Plymouth Reliant "K" sedan Chief's car serving the Dwight D. Eisenhower Veterans Affairs Medical Center Fire Department in Leavenworth, Kansas. This car had a transverse-mounted, 84-horsepower four-cylinder engine and a 99.6-inch wheelbase. Photo courtesy Steve Loftin collection

This white over yellow Chief's car is a 1980s Plymouth Gran Fury sedan assigned to the Yukon Fire Department, Oklahoma. This Plymouth model was the counterpart to the Dodge Diplomat. Photo courtesy Steve Loftin collection

This scenic shot of a 1983 Chevrolet Malibu sedan is a Battalion Chief's car serving San Francisco, California. Note the painted wheels on this white over red car. Photo courtesy Bill Egan

Another government fire department using a Plymouth "K" car. The Chief of the Great Lakes Naval Training Center in Illinois was assigned this white with red striped 1985 station wagon. Photo courtesy Racine Firebell Museum Association

Fort Monmouth, New Jersey, provided a bright yellow (with maroon interior!) 1987 Chevrolet Corsica for its Fire Chief. Note the dash-mounted warning light. Photo courtesy Arthur Knobloch

The 1980s also saw tremendous sales growth of four-wheel-drive vehicles. Many models such as the Jeep Wagoneer and the Ford Bronco had been produced since the 1960s, but their acceptance by the city and town fire departments took a while. The general public liked what they saw, and automakers geared up to produce more and more four-wheel-drive vehicles. The forests, mountains, and rural hills and valleys were the proving grounds for the Scouts and Suburbans of the Forest Service and Mountain VFD. What follows is a sampling of the Chief vehicles in the "4WD" category.

The AMC Jeep Cherokee by 1983 had a completely new body and dropped 1,000 pounds of weight for better performance. The Baltimore City Fire Department in Maryland had a fleet of these four-wheel-drive Chief's wagons. Photo courtesy Arthur Knobloch

This 1985 Chevrolet Blazer was assigned to the East Battalion Chief in New Haven, Connecticut. Car 33 was painted white.

The red 1985 Chevrolet Silverado Chief's unit serving Tulsa, Oklahoma. Cost $10,579 without options. Photo courtesy Steve Loftin collection

A white over red with white striped 1987 Chevrolet Blazer provided for the Battalion Chief of the Portage, Michigan Fire Department. Photo courtesy Daniel Jasina

A red 1987 Chevrolet Scottsdale serving the Richmond, Virginia, Bureau of Fire as a Battalion Chief's vehicle. Photo courtesy R.D. Jennings

A white over red 1989-91 Chevrolet Suburban (2500 series) Battalion Chief's wagon at a fire scene in Tempe, Arizona. This unit has amber and red warning lights. Photo courtesy Steve Cloutier

Another white over red 1989-91 Chevrolet Suburban (2500 series), this one assigned to FDNY Rescue Operations. Note the heavy-duty chrome grille guard up front.

Beginning with the second series 1955 models and continuing through the 1980s, General Motors also built Suburbans under the GMC banner. This 1981 Sierra was used at Coney Island by the FDNY 43rd Battalion Chief. Photo courtesy Jack Calderone

A white 1985-86 GMC Sierra used by the Community Fire Company of Franklin Township in New Jersey. This Incident Command Vehicle, Car 25, carries a fancy red and blue stripe design. Cost $13,996.

A red 1988-89 GMC 1500 series (half ton) assigned to the Katonah, New York Fire Department. Cost $14,996. Car 2211 features graphics that emulates the vintage gold leaf-style trim. Photo courtesy Ron Bogardus

GMC named this 4X4 Jimmy. The 1989 Model S-15 is the officer of the day "buggy" for the BWI Airport Fire Department. The Jimmy is light yellow with a white mid-stripe color. The Federal Model 24 Aerodynic roof mount gets your attention. Photo courtesy John D. Floyd, Jr.

The Ford Bronco (its production run beginning in 1966) was backed into many fire stations during the 1980s with Chief logos affixed to its sides. The following is a sampling of the many that were used by the fire service during the decade.

A bright yellow 1985 Bronco Battalion Chief's 4X4 serving Camden, New Jersey. Note the aftermarket "runningboards." Photo courtesy Arthur Knobloch

A white with gold striped late-1980s Bronco XLT Asst. Chief's 4X4 assigned to the Ridgeway Volunteer Fire Company in Manchester Township, New Jersey. The roof bar is a Federal Streethawk. Photo courtesy William Schwartz

This red over white 1989 Bronco XLT 4x4 is on duty with the Queenstown Volunteer Fire Department, Maryland. Chief 3 has custom warning lights mounted in its grille. Photo courtesy John D. Floyd, Jr.

The Dodge Division of Chrysler built cars, trucks and vans in the 1980s. This decade's photographs began with the Dodge Diplomat and will end with a sampling of the different types of Dodge vehicles the fire service has purchased during the 1980s.

This 1980 Dodge Power Wagon was a U.S. Navy Asst. Fire Chief's vehicle supporting our troops and the fire department at Guantanamo Bay, Cuba. This chrome yellow pickup carried 12 pressurized water extinguishers and a CO2 unit. Note the heavy-duty grille guard. Photo courtesy James Derstine

A late-1980s Ram B150 window van assigned to the Special Service Unit of the Liberty Corner, New Jersey Fire Company. Its Chief was attending fire school at the New York City Fire Academy.

Pittsburgh, Pennsylvania, adopted its football Steelers' team colors of black and yellow for its fire vehicles in the 1980s. This Dodge Ram Charger is the Battalion No. 6 Chief's 4X4. Photo courtesy John Schmidt

Another late-1980s Dodge Ram cargo van used by the Springfield State Hospital Fire Department in Maryland. The Chief uses the van as Car 1. Photo courtesy Steve Hagy

Dodge's Ram Charger was a 4X4 with V-8 power. Battalion Chief No. 1 of the St. Louis, Missouri Fire Department was provided this go-everywhere vehicle. Aftermarket aluminum "runningboards" have been added to aid that first step. Photo courtesy Steve Hagy

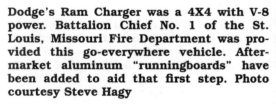

THE BIGGEST AND THE BEST: 1990-1999

The 1990s saw improvements in automobile design, economy, performance, and size. Based on the vast number of different models available, it was quite evident that the four-wheel-drive vehicles were here to stay. The long-running, rear-drive Ford Crown Victoria and Chevrolet Caprice sedans were solid competitors for most of the decade. Chevrolet ended Caprice production in 1996, but the Ford "Crown Vic" will be available for police and fire departments into the 21st century. Vehicle choices increased during the decade including minivans from all the manufacturers, and models such as the Chevrolet Tahoe and Ford Explorer and Expedition. Marketing devised a new name for four-wheel-drive vehicles, SUV (sport utility vehicle), and the public bought them for everyday driving. Ford introduced its Excursion in late-1999, a competitor to the Chevrolet and GMC Suburban. Option lists kept growing and giving the fire departments more choices. The electronic age led to design improvements that made accessories fun. The 4X4s could be shifted by pushing a button, doors could be locked and unlocked by pushing a remote button, and emergency help was available when airbags were deployed or directions were needed—you guessed it—by pushing the OnStar button.

We entered the 20th century with the Fire Chief holding the reins to his horse while the "Buggy" or "Wagon" carried him to the fire. We enter the 21st century with the Chief surrounded by a steel cage, belted to a heated-cushion seat, assisted by power controls, listening to audible messages and warnings, carrying advanced cutting/prying tools and equipment that aids in the breathing of clean air or zaps new life into a human. The next Chief car purchased will have the reverse ultrasonic sensing system that alerts the driver when backing to objects behind the vehicle. It may save the life of a child who, someday, could grow up to be a Fire Chief!

The following photographs are a representative group of Chief vehicles that best illustrate the modern fire service of the late-20th century.

This Fire Department "portrait" shows the Chief's car and apparatus of the Morningside (Maryland) Volunteer Fire Department. The photo was taken during the department's 50th anniversary in 1995. Each piece of equipment carries the name of a well-known manufacturer: (L-R) Dodge Chief's car, 1995 Pierce 1250, 1990 Seagrave 1250, 1995 HME/Saulsbury Rescue, 1986 Chevrolet/Haz-mat. Photo courtesy John D. Floyd, Jr.

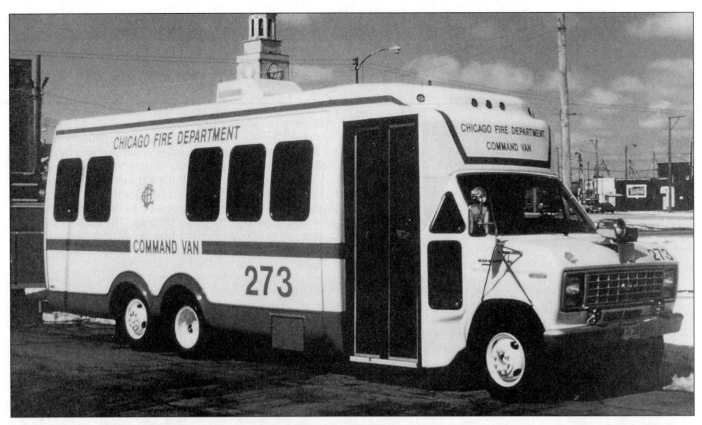

The Chicago, Illinois Fire Department has several generations of command vehicles. This 1990 Ford Starstran van is one of four Incident Command Vans. It's the Chief's field office on wheels. Photo courtesy Hank Sajovic

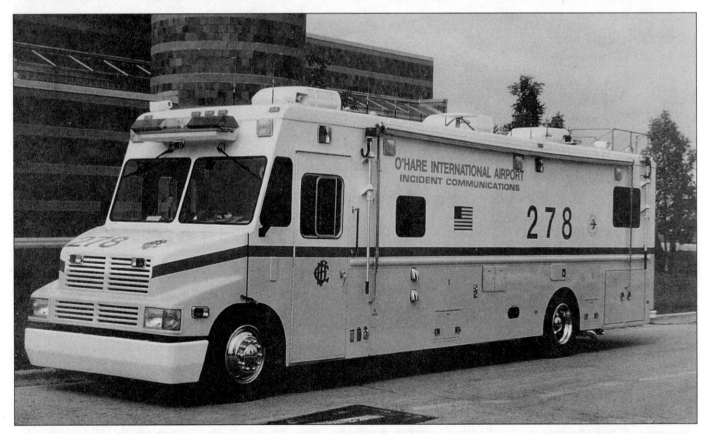

Chicago O'Hare International Airport in Illinois uses this 1994 Navistar/LTV for its Incident Command Van. This van would respond to all aircraft crashes in the city and within a 25-mile radius of O'Hare Field. The FAA could order it to any incident, as a Command Center. Photo courtesy Hank Sajovic

This 1991 Dodge Caravan is the first of a new series of minivans from Chrysler. This Chief's van is from the Great Lakes Naval Training Center near Chicago, Illinois. Minivan features include airbags installed in the steering wheel for driver safety as well as rear seats that can be folded or removed altogether for extra cargo room. Photo courtesy Racine Firebell Museum Association

This Asst. Fire Chief's van is a Dodge Grand Caravan with extended cargo space. Chrysler led the industry in minivan sales during the 1990s. This plain white Dodge is a U.S. Government van for the Fort Leavenworth, Kansas Fire Department. Photo courtesy Steve Loftin collection

Chrysler Corp.'s newest minivan series began with the 1996 model and continued through the decade. These minivans were offered through Chrysler, Dodge, or Plymouth dealers. In addition to the standard four-cylinder engine, optional powerplants included a 3.0-liter V-6, 3.3-liter V-6, or 3.8-liter V-6. Manchester, Connecticut, purchased this Dodge Caravan to aid and assist fire rescue operations. Photo courtesy Richard Bartlett

The Dodge Ram Charger 4X4 continued into the 1990s with this grille design for the 1991-92 model year. The Chief from the Neptune City, New Jersey Fire Department was attending a muster with his 4X4. The Federal Streethawk emergency light bar backs up the strobe and speakers up front.

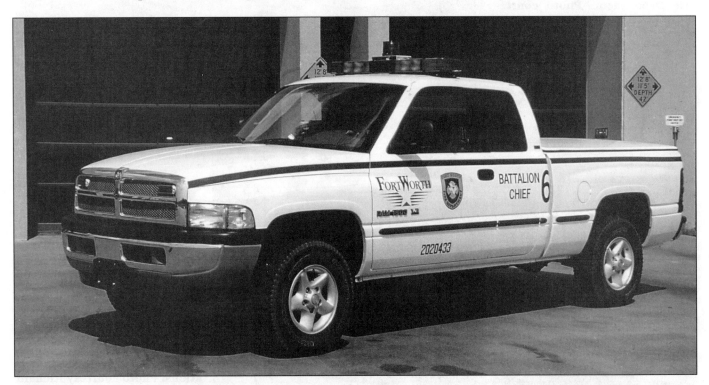

Dodge trucks introduced a new design in 1995. This 1998 club cab pickup is a 4X4 Ram Model 1500. The 6th Battalion Chief from Fort Worth, Texas Fire Department drives this white "Wagon" on his shift. Factory options include a V-10 engine. Photo courtesy Eric Hansen

After purchasing American Motors in the late-1980s, Chrysler Corp. continued Jeep production into the 1990s. This 4X4 Jeep is provided for the Fire Chief from King of Prussia, Pennsylvania. The black over red paint matches the wheels and grille. Note the door logo and the white lettered tires. Photo courtesy James Derstine

Battalion Chief's red Jeep Cherokee from Baltimore City Fire Department, Maryland. The door logo reads "Pride Protecting People." Photo courtesy John D. Floyd, Jr.

Safety Officer's Jeep serving the Baltimore City Fire Department, Maryland. The vehicle is white with an orange center stripe. Photo courtesy John D. Floyd, Jr.

The Battalion Chief and his Jeep Cherokee assigned to the Salisbury, North Carolina Fire Department. Note the Pirsch ladder truck that dwarfs the Jeep.

The 1997 Jeep Cherokee featured a new grille and corner lights but remained chromeless. This white Asst. Chief's 4X4 "Wagon" serves the DDRE at New Cumberland, Pennsylvania. It has county, aircraft, and base radios. The red side stripes and lettering are decals. Photo courtesy James Derstine

A white Jeep 4X4 used by the Chief for the Naval District of Washington, D.C. The art of gold leafing for insignia logos and striping on fire vehicles has been replaced by computer-generated decals and reflective stripes.

The full-size Chevrolet Caprice continued to be a favorite with metro fire departments during the 1990s.

White over red with white striped Caprice Asst. Chief's car serving the Kenosha, Wisconsin Fire Department.

Black over red Caprice Deputy District Chief's car from Chicago, Illinois. Photo courtesy Gordon J. Nord, Jr.

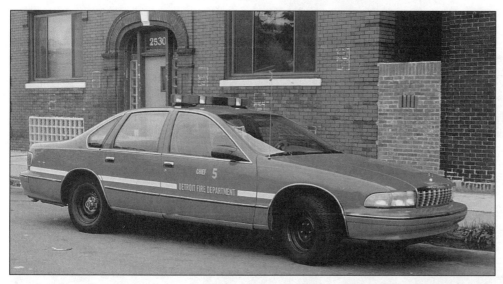

Red with white striped Caprice Chief's car assigned to the Detroit, Michigan Fire Department. Note no hubcaps! Photo courtesy Walt McCall

White Caprice Chief's car serving the Mountain Home Volunteer Fire Department, Idaho. Note the "flames" painted behind each wheel well and the fire and rescue crash trucks of the Mountain Home AFB displayed in the background. Photo courtesy Don P. Abrahamson

Black with thin red striped Caprice assigned to Fire Commissioner Raymond Orozco of the Chicago, Illinois Fire Department. Note that there are no markings or lettering on the car, but check out the walls in the background! Photo courtesy Hank Sajovic

This is the Chief Duty Officer of the Day for New York City, with his chauffeured Caprice. The Chief is the Division One Commander. FDNY cars are white over red with chrome yellow and white reflective stripes.

A Chevrolet Caprice station wagon with a fold-down rear seat. This dark red wagon is assigned to the New Hampshire State Fire Marshal. Photo courtesy Box 388 Productions

A 1995 Chevrolet command van serving the Forest Bend Volunteer Fire Department, near Houston, Texas. This white with red striped minivan gives the Chief plenty of utility space. Photo courtesy William Wilcox

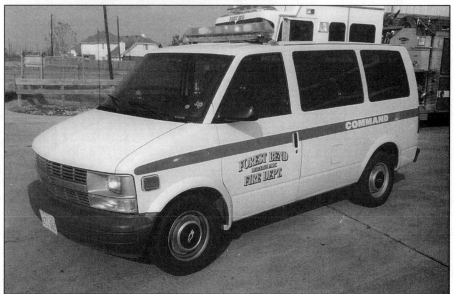

Many Chevrolet pickups are used by fire departments for repair and shop supply, but this 1990s 2500 series club cab truck is used by the Chief for responding to alarms. Charlestown is in Cecil County, Maryland. Photo courtesy John D. Floyd, Jr.

Chief Ken Hetrick and his Chevrolet Blazer S-10 in front of Fire Headquarters at West Point Military Academy in New York. S-10 production took place from 1983-1993. This 4X4 featured a 100.5-inch wheelbase and was powered by a 4.3-liter engine rated at 165 horsepower.

The Deputy Chief of the Atlantic City, New Jersey Fire Department was provided with this 1990s Chevrolet Blazer 1500 series 4X4. The Blazer is red with dual white stripes. Photo courtesy John D. Floyd, Jr.

Chief's "Buggy" on duty at Maui County, Hawaii, Station No. 10. This fire department Chevrolet Blazer with emergency light bar is assigned to the shift commander. All the vehicles and apparatus at the Kahului, Maui Island station are pineapple yellow in color. I wonder why? This full-size Blazer will be a two-door Tahoe SUV by the end of the decade.

The last half of the 1990s found a rounded-front Chevrolet full-size Suburban look-alike, with a shorter wheelbase. This Boston (Massachusetts) District Commander's unit is a Tahoe 1500 series and is red with a white center stripe. Note the serious-looking front bumper guard. Photo courtesy John M. Calderone

This Tahoe Chief's vehicle is assigned to the Trenton, New Jersey Fire Department. It is white over red with white and chrome yellow striping. The safety message on the rear window reads "Did You Test Your Smoke Detector Lately?"

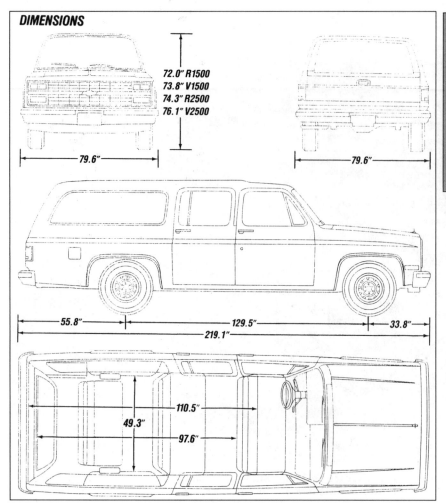

DIMENSIONS

72.0" R1500
73.8" V1500
74.3" R2500
76.1" V2500

79.6"

79.6"

55.8"   129.5"   33.8"

219.1"

110.5"

49.3"   97.6"

The most popular vehicle (by photo count) used in the 1990s as a Chief's "Buggy" is the Chevrolet and GMC Suburban. General Motors made a major change in the Suburban's body in 1992. Its wheelbase and all dimensions were revised. All the fire departments had to do was add their logos, insignias, and reflecting stripes, top it with a light bar, and fill the cargo space with fire fighting gear. The two photos compare before and after measurements.

The Suburban's dimensions and design before 1992.

The Suburban's dimensions and design after 1992.

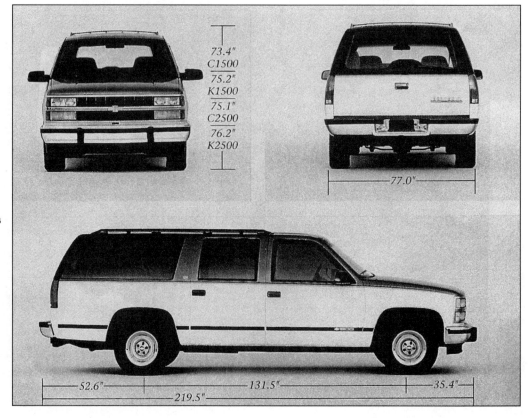

73.4"
C1500
75.2"
K1500
75.1"
C2500
76.2"
K2500

77.0"

52.6"   131.5"   35.4"

219.5"

A sample of Chevrolet Suburbans used as Chief's vehicles. All have emergency light bars from various manufacturers: Code III, Whelen, Federal, Unity, and Dietz, to name a few.

Early-1990s Suburban from Nantucket Island Fire Department, Massachusetts. It's white over red with chrome yellow door lettering. Photo courtesy Box 388 Productions

Winston-Salem, North Carolina Fire Department Incident Commander Leroy Davis with his mid-1990s Suburban equipped with a bounce-back Duragrille. The interior shot of a modern Chief's vehicle shows the array of computer equipment needed to do the job.

A mid-1990s 1500 series Suburban on duty with the Lumberton Fire Company, New Jersey. The unit is red with a white stripe and is equipped with aftermarket runningboards. Photo courtesy the late Jim Burner collection

The Garland, Texas Fire Department provided its Battalion Chief this 1996 Suburban. The 2500 series "Buggy" is white over red and features a Duragrille. Photo courtesy Eric Hansen

Braircliff Manor, New York Fire Department's late-1990s Suburban 2500 series. It's white with gold leaf trim and lettering, aftermarket runningboards and bumper guard, and Duragrille. Photo courtesy Ron Bogardus

Reminiscent of a 1950s custom car with a "flame job," Garfield, New Jersey Fire Department's Chief's "Wagon" is a white 1993 Suburban 1500 series that sports gold flames and stripe. Note dual light bars on top of roof. Photo courtesy Arthur Knobloch

Grand Rapids, Michigan Fire Department's 1994 Suburban 1500 series provided for its Battalion Chief. It's white over red with chrome yellow lettering. Photo courtesy Daniel Jasina

Mid-1990s Suburban 2500 series Chief's vehicle serving the U.S. Air Force, Stewart AFB, New York. It's blue with white stripes and is equipped with a Duragrille.

General Motors also built GMC Suburbans as a mirror image of the Chevrolet version. Many of the city fire departments preferred the GMC "Wagon." These heavy-duty vehicles are the carry-all, do-all units that the modern Fire Chief needs to provide for public safety. The sampling shown represents a few of the many different configurations of paint and trim found on Chief's Suburbans in fire departments all over this nation.

Mount Pleasant, Wisconsin Fire Department's early-1990s 2500 series 4X4. The unit is white with a red stripe. Photo courtesy Racine Firebell Museum Association

A 1993 2500 series Battalion Chief's "Wagon" on duty with the Los Angeles City Fire Department, California. It's white over red. Photo courtesy Daniel Jasina

Plainfield, New Jersey Fire Department's mid-1990s 1500 series Deputy Chief's vehicle. It's white with red stripe package and silver maltese badge. Photo courtesy John M. Calderone

Philadelphia, Pennsylvania Fire Department's 1995 2500 series 4X4 Battalion Chief's "Buggy." It's white over red with chrome yellow and white stripes. Interior shot shows almost aircraft-quality communications console. Photos courtesy William Schwartz

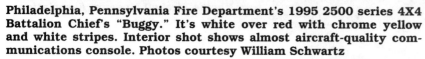

Vehicle GM9446 is the FDNY 23rd Battalion Chief's unit. It's white over red with chrome yellow and white reflective stripes and lettering. New York Chief's "Wagons" have super light and sound warning systems. Note the series of lights on the rear roof. This is an electrically operated double arm mechanism, which raises to form a "U" shape set of flashing lights at the fire scene. Photo courtesy John M. Calderone

Memphis, Tennessee Fire Department's red 1995 1500 series Battalion Chief's vehicle with a Duragrille. Photo courtesy William Schwartz

General Motors also offered a smaller four-door SUV with four-wheel-drive. This Chief's vehicle is a 1996 GMC Jimmy assigned to the North Bergen, New Jersey Fire Department. All the automakers would have sport utility vehicles available by the end of the decade. Photo courtesy Arthur Knobloch

The Ford Crown Victoria sedan continued seeing duty as a Chief's car throughout the 1990s. The following photos are a sampling of paint and trim configurations seen on modern "Crown Vics."

Odenton (Maryland) Volunteer Fire Department's Chief's Crown Victoria. This 1990 model was the last of the "square" body design. It's white over red with gold striping. Photo courtesy John D. Floyd, Jr.

A new generation of Crown Victoria started with the 1991 model. This is the 3rd Battalion Chief's "Crown Vic" assigned to the Atlanta, Georgia Fire Department. It's white over red. Photo courtesy John D. Floyd, Jr.

Late-1990s Crown Victoria features a new grille. The District Chief from Worcester, Massachusetts Fire Department drives this white with red and shades of red striped car. Photo courtesy Dick Bartlett

Detroit, Michigan Fire Department's Chief uses this yellow late-1990s Crown Victoria while on duty. Photo courtesy Walt McCall

During the 1990s, the Ford Bronco was another popular Chief's vehicle due to its four-wheel-drive utility. The following photos are a sampling of the East Coast departments' Broncos.

Early-1990s Bronco serving the Lebanon Bureau of Fire, Pennsylvania. It's predominantly red with a white stripe.

Fire Chief's 1994 Bronco assigned to the U.S. Army Fire Department protecting the Military Ocean Terminal in Bayonne, New Jersey. Another red with white striped example. Photo courtesy John M. Calderone

White with red striped Deputy Chief's Bronco XLT on duty with the Quincy, Massachusetts Fire Department. Full frontal protection bar is added to the heavy-duty grille guard. Note the "dress" accessory bug shield. Photo courtesy Box 388 Productions

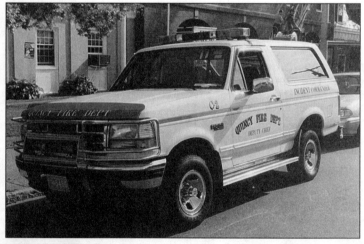

Fire Chief's Bronco XLT serving the Fort Dix, New Jersey Fire Department. The red Ford features black and chrome yellow custom decals and white lettered tires. For military fire equipment, this is quite a departure from the more traditional olive drab. Photo courtesy James Derstine

The Ford Explorer represented a growth trend among buyers in the 1990s. The features of this type of short-wheelbase vehicle, including optional four-wheel-drive, helped sales to the general public as well as the fire service for use as a Chief's vehicle. Fire departments in the early-1990s used Explorers such as the following examples.

Friendswood (Texas) Volunteer Fire Department. It's red with a white stripe. Photo courtesy William Wilcox

Idaho Falls, Idaho Fire Department. It's bright yellow with gold leaf logos and black lettering. Photo courtesy Deran Watt

Defense Distribution Regional Center Public Safety Unit, New Cumberland, Pennsylvania. It's white with a red stripe. Photo courtesy James Derstine

Ford continued the Explorer into the late-1990s with a new body style. This new-look example is assigned to the Deputy Chief of the Atlantic City, New Jersey Fire Department. It's white with a red reflector stripe. Photo courtesy the late Jim Burner collection

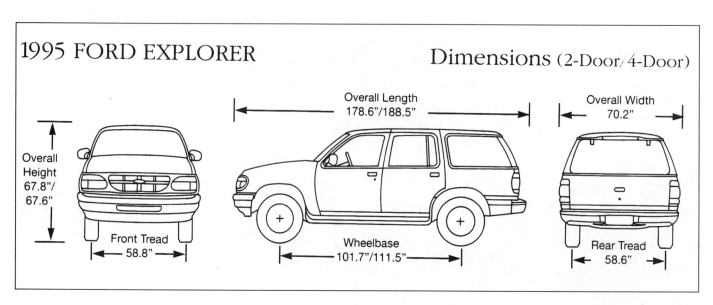

1995 FORD EXPLORER   Dimensions (2-Door/4-Door)

Overall Length
178.6"/188.5"

Overall Width
70.2"

Overall
Height
67.8"/
67.6"

Front Tread
58.8"

Wheelbase
101.7"/111.5"

Rear Tread
58.6"

Ford's heavy-duty hauler for both passengers and cargo is the Expedition. The four-wheel-drive option is just one of many available. The fire service will be using this model well into the 21st century, as the following examples show.

Chief's Car 50 from the South Plainfield, New Jersey Fire Department. Custom stripes and insignia are computer cut. Photo courtesy John M. Calderone

Command 1 from Lincoln, Ontario, Canada, was the first Expedition used in Canada for fire fighting duty. It was delivered March 13, 1998. Photo courtesy Walt McCall

This 1999 Ford Expedition is Car 48 assigned to the Chief of the Hershey, Pennsylvania Fire Department—home of the Milton Hershey School and the Hershey Chocolate Co. The school's Founders Hall is in the background. The white with red striped Ford has a Federal Signal emergency light bar and deflector shield on the hood.

A 1999 Ford Expedition Chief's vehicle serving the Middlebush VFD, Franklin Township, Somerset County, New Jersey. District 1's Chief was visiting the Fire Expo in Harrisburg, Pennsylvania. This Expedition was professionally outfitted on delivery. It's white with red and chrome yellow striping and red and black lettering.

This final section presented the best of the modern vehicles used by the fire service. At this very moment, automakers are hard at work designing new and better vehicles for the 21st century. One such manufacturer is Ford, which will introduce a year 2000 vehicle that has potential for use in the fire service.

Ford's heavy-duty performer is off the drawing board and ready to offer to fire service buyers. The vehicle is called Excursion. It's a nine-passenger, super-size cargo carrier. It's 7.2 inches longer then the Chevrolet Suburban, with a 5.6-inch longer wheelbase. The three engine choices are: 5.4-liter V-8 rated at 260 horsepower, a 6.8-liter V-10 rated at 300 horsepower, and a 7.3-liter diesel V-8 rated at 235 horsepower. The comparison charts have some awesome numbers, as will the Excursion's price tag!

RESTORED

You may find restored Fire Chief cars in museums, at musters, and in private collections. These cars are restored and in fine running order, but may have never seen duty as a Chief's Buggy. It would be hard to emulate a fire apparatus, based on its size and complex workings, but an antique automobile is different. The addition of lights, siren, and lettering after a total restoration will permit the owner to live in the past without direct ties to the fire service.

The situation could also be reversed. After purchasing a used 25-year veteran fire chief car at a city auction, the car could be restored to its showroom configuration. The act, in both cases, preserves automotive history. Due to the immense size of antique fire apparatus and the need for large facilities to store it, the fire buffs of the future will more and more be turning their attention to Chief cars to enjoy the hobby.

What follows is a sampling of the many Fire Chief cars kept alive and running.

(Left) This 1908 Cadillac is from Old Forge Fire Department, in the State of New York. The car may not be a Chief's car, but to find any fire car made before 1910 makes it worthy of viewing.

American LaFrance built this roadster in 1911 as a race car. It was restored by Figgie International and may be viewed in the North Carolina Factory Museum of American LaFrance. It has been advertised as the last surviving Chief's car, but was never recorded as being used by the fire service. Photo courtesy Daniel Jasina

A 1912 Selden Model 47 Chief's car shown while in service in New York state. It was later purchased by Harrah's Automobile Collection and restored to its original configuration in 1971. This Chief's car may be viewed today at the National Auto Museum, Reno, Nevada. Factory price $2,500. It was equipped with a 40-horsepower four-cylinder engine, and a "Northeast" starter (front of radiator). Selden automobiles were built in Rochester, New York, until 1914. Photo courtesy Robert Potter

A 1914 Saxon roadster used by the Fremont (Nebraska) Fire Company for parades and show. It, also, is not recorded as being a Chief's car.

A 1915 Model T Ford Chief's car from the collection of the late Henry Austin Clark, Jr. This postcard was sold at his Long Island Auto Museum. Mr. Clark was an author and collector of antique automobiles.

This 1916 Model T Ford Chief's car is exhibited at musters by the Southampton Fire Company of Long Island, New York.

A 1916 Model T Ford Chief's car outfitted by American LaFrance for the Niagara Fire Company of Merchantville, New Jersey.

This FDNY Model T Ford Chief's car shown on the street, before its restoration was completed. The maltese plate has an "M" in the center. The inset view is of the car with the gold leaf trim and lettering after restoration. The car is on display in the FDNY maintenance shops.

A 1927 Model T Ford Chief's car owned by Jim Golden of Bowie, Maryland. The car was delivered to Lille, Maine, in June of 1927, and was in service until 1947. It passed through several hands before Golden bought it in 1980. Apparatus manufacturer Obenchain-Boyer performed the modifications on the Ford chassis. Golden has given it a lot of TLC!

Fire Chief pickup at SPAAMFAA Muster.

Model A Fords have always been a favorite with car buffs. Fire buffs are no exception, and many Model As are seen at parades and fire musters. Shown are six Model A cars witnessed at parades or musters:

Fire Prevention Chief. Photo courtesy Steve Cloutier

1928 Model A owned by Elaine Ferraro. Photo courtesy John D. Floyd, Jr.

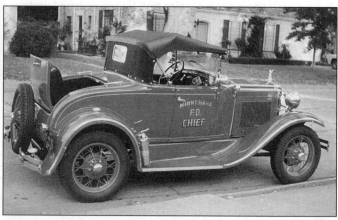

1931 Model A Ford roadster, from Stockton, California. A private owner purchased the car locally, restored it and painted it red, with lettering for his own fire company name of "Minnehaha." Photo courtesy Edward Christopher

1929 Model A of Yardley-Makefield Fire Co. No. 1 of Yardley, Pennsylvania. It took members of the company four years to restore this Model A. Photo courtesy James T. Coyne

Myerstown, Pennsylvania, Model A with Chief Shaak.

A restored 1929 Model A Ford Tudor sedan, owned by Al Lignelli, of Ellicott City, Maryland. This picture was taken at a Pennsylvania Pump Primers Muster, in Harrisburg, Pennsylvania. The Mars light fastened to the bumper is an expensive item, compared to the original cost of the car ($525). Photo courtesy John Schmidt

The Newtown Antique Fire Association (NAFA) has its 1936 Ford Chief's car ready to lead its apparatus in a parade. Photo courtesy William Witt

The Pierce Manufacturing Co., of Appleton, Wisconsin, restored this 1935 Ford coupe with all the bells and lights possible to parade and advertise its products. Photo courtesy Arthur Knobloch

Howard L. Brenner of Riverwoods, Illinois, replicated a 1935 Ford five-window coupe to the specifications of a previous "Buggy" that ran out of Engine Co. 68 on Chicago's northwest side. He did a fine job, right down to the green and red headlight lenses. Photo courtesy Howard L. Brenner

A clean 1937 Chevrolet coupe at a muster, with simple maltese cross and a fender-mounted siren. Photo courtesy Wayne Kidd

This World War II jeep was restored by William Wilcox of Friendswood, Texas. The 1945 Willys Overland was stationed at Camp Hulen Army Airfield at Palacios, Texas. Besides the equipment shown, there is a water pump can inside and a siren on the right fender. Photo courtesy William Wilcox

This restored 1948 Ford Chief's buggy is from Iron Mountain (Michigan) Fire Department. It shows up at parades and musters, driven by its private owner.

An unusual car for the Fire Chief is this 1948 Ford "woodie" station wagon from Atascadero, California. This Super Deluxe wagon cost $1,972 new without the warning lights and siren. The spotlight doubles as a warning light. Photo courtesy Ed Haas

A bright red 1948 Plymouth at a New York muster. The license plate ensures '48 vintage with a faded Milltown on the maltese cross. A polished brass bell and a Federal 66L siren round out the antique look. Photo courtesy Scott Schimpf

This 1949 Plymouth four-door sedan has been restored by Ray Pitts of Beverly, Massachusetts. Pitts used the paint design and proper equipment to emulate a Chicago Chief's buggy. Photo courtesy John Schmidt

A restored 1951 Chrysler Club Coupe parading at the Greenfield Village Muster in Michigan. Photo courtesy Richard L. Story

A 1951 Packard Patrician 400 from the Fire Brigade of the Packard Motor Co. plant. The Fire Chief used the best to protect the rest! Photo courtesy James Derstine

William Cary of Rome, New York, restored this 1951 Ford Deluxe former Chief's car from the Wellsburg (New York) Fire Department. Cary uses his car for musters and fire buffing. Photo courtesy William Cary

John Schmidt of Mount Lebanon, Pennsylvania, restored this 1951 Chevrolet Chief's car. Siren and red light were original. Photo courtesy John Schmidt

Wayne Kidd, shown with his restored 1953 Ford Chief's car. Kidd is from Mechanicsville, Virginia. This car has all the equipment from the 1950 Cold War era, and was built to emulate a vehicle from the City of Richmond, Virginia. Photo courtesy Wayne Kidd

Bob Muller from Tempe, Arizona, restored this 1954 Chevrolet sedan. The bold initials on the hood are typical of the apparatus painting of that era. Photo courtesy Bob Muller

John Fuller of Sparks, Nevada, restored his 1954 Packard hardtop into a Chief's car. Fuller is a former fire fighter, and got the okay from the local fire department to use its decals and lettering, and then added a beacon and siren to complete the project. He drives it in local parades and to car shows and fire prevention demonstrations. Photo courtesy John Schmidt

A SPAAMFAA National Muster display included this 1955 Willys Aero, white over red with whitewall tires. A sporty looking car for a small fire company. Photo courtesy James Derstine

A restored 1957 DeSoto station wagon marked for the New Kensington Fire Company No.3 in Maryland. The card in the windshield indicates the owner is showing the Chief's car at an event. Photo courtesy Steve Cloutier

This restored 1959 Ford station wagon was part of a muster in Salisbury, Maryland. Fruitland Volunteer Fire Company is located near Salisbury. White over red color was a popular combination. Photo courtesy John D. Floyd, Jr.

This restored 1961 Chevrolet Impala was found parked in front of the Wheaton Village entrance, in New Jersey. Fire musters are held there annually. The black roof holds a host of warning devices, including a double tone siren and beacon light.

Ford built these compact cars during the 1960s, and this restored Falcon sedan was found at a muster in Greenfield Village, Michigan. It is a former Birmingham City Fire Department car assigned to the fire marshal. Photo courtesy Richard L. Story

Fire museums all over the world commonly feature a particularly unusual piece of apparatus, but seldom a Chief's car. The Speyer Museum in Germany displays this 300D Mercedes Saloon blue light special. Cost DM 27,000 (approximately $14,300). Photo courtesy James Derstine

Steve Cloutier of Weddington, North Carolina, restored this 1963 Ford Galaxie from the Carmel Fire Department. A matching red interior sets off the dividing chrome of the exterior. The standard items delivered to the fire company still grace the Chief car. Photo courtesy Steve Cloutier

A former San Francisco Battalion Chief "Buggy," owned by Del and Connie Lindstrom of Livermore, California. The 1965 Ford sedan is displayed with a professional easel board. Events featuring this type of display help the public understand the heritage of the fire service. Photo courtesy Ed Haas

Brad Harper restored this 1973 Dodge Polara, a former Chapel Hill, North Carolina Fire Department Chief car, to the specifications of a Phoenix, Arizona, Chief car. Harper lives in Atkins, Iowa. Photo courtesy Brad Harper.

FIRE CHIEF CAR COLLECTIBLES

Mention the word "collectible" to enthusiasts of the fire memorabilia hobby and they would visualize different things. Polished bells and antique hose nozzles may be on one person's collectible list, while fire truck toys may be another person's desire.

This book is a photographic history of fire chief cars, and it's only natural to include the collecting of toys and models that imitate the real thing. Because the automobile had such a large impact on the toy industry, toy makers were hard at work after the Chief cars answered their first alarm. The fire department cars raced to the fires, just like the horses. It was exciting in the minds of children, so the toy makers identified the toy cars with "FD" or "Fire Chief" to help market their wares. Small children and parents alike could relate to these toy cars marked with "Fire Chief," and fantasize by making their own sounds for loud exhaust and ringing bells.

These toys would be passed down through the generations to become the collectibles of today. Toy makers continued to produce look-alike "Fire Chief" cars as the automakers annually changed the outward appearance of their cars.

Materials for the toys also changed. Cast iron fire toys made at the turn of century are prized as highly as any first edition. Cast iron, wood, steel, tin metal, plastic, pot metal, and even rubber have been used for these toys. Today, a combination of materials is common in many of the better toys and models. Tin toys were a favorite with several toy makers, such as Marx, because tin was easy to paint, bend and assemble.

Wind-up mechanisms added for motion helped to make these toys more realistic. The addition of lights and siren noises, powered by dry cell batteries, improved play action enormously. The toy season for the last several years has included "Fire Chief" cars and vans with microchip voices and/or sounds, at the push of a button. These toys from the beginning were meant to be played with, by children, and can be found in any condition from pristine to stressed.

Fire chief car collectibles of the scale model variety are normally purchased to shelve. They are made to exacting scale, and carry the smallest detail to the highest degree. These are not considered toys for children's play, and may never see the light of day. Some are purchased as kits, others are complete with the decals in place. A few are molded glass decanters.

Fire buffs and collectors alike see these toys and models as a link to bring back memories and create a feeling of nostalgia. The toys and models of fire chief cars on the following pages are examples found in the world of collecting.

1910-1920 roadster, cast iron. Harry Rosenblum

1920s coupe, cast iron, Arcade. *Old Cars Weekly* file

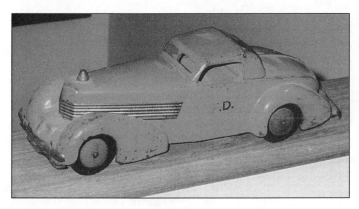

1936-37 Cord coupe, steel. Harry Rosenblum

Plastic wind-up, 3-5/8-inch length, Jimson, made in Hong Kong.

Plastic wind-up. *Old Cars Weekly* file

1960 Lincoln, bump'n go, battery-operated flashing light and siren noise. Yonezawa Toys LTD.

Tin toy wind-up. *Old Cars Weekly* file

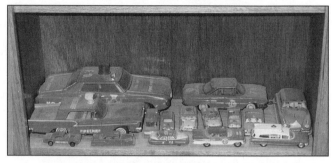

Part of a collector's parking garage. Harry Rosenblum

1940s Hudson, plastic wind-up, with battery light. Harry Rosenblum

Steel van, Tonka, five-inch length.

1968 Toronado, tin, with battery and motor, mystery bump'n go.

Steel Jeep wagon, Tonka, Fire Chief No. 1066, 9-1/4-inch length.

Hot Wheels, Mattel five pack-fire fighting, die cast 3-inch length.

Mattel First Wheels, push toy, 3-inch length, made in Hong Kong.

Matchbox, Jeep Cherokee, part of a five pack, die cast 2-3/4-inch length.

1964 Ford, plastic, red and blue, manufactured for Grants.

Road Rough cars, box of 12 (five fire fighting), die cast, pull back action, 4-1/2-inch length. Made in China.

1959 Ford tin toy, with box, made in Japan. *Old Cars Weekly* file

Action City play set, fire chief car, by Real Toy, 2-7/8-inch length.

1997 Dodge pickup, City Force, plastic, 13-1/2-inch length, light and sound.

1997 Ford Explorer, City Force, plastic, 9-inch length, light and sound.

1997 Chevrolet Tahoe, City Force, plastic, 13-1/2-inch length, light and sound.

1997 GMC Suburban, City Force, plastic, 13-1/2-inch length, light and sound.

Scale Models

Scale models can be found for sale anyplace fire fighters gather for an event. Fire expos and musters have flea markets where models are sold.

1957 Chevrolet, Road Legend No. 19, 1/18 scale, made in China. Scott Schimpf

1936 Ford coupe, The 43rd Ave. Collection, 1/43 scale, made in England. Scott Schimpf

Model A Ford pickup, FDNY searchlight equipped, Models of Yesteryear. Scott Schimpf

1940 Ford, Division of Motor City of California, 1/43 scale. Scott Schimpf

1941 Packard, Brothers model, 1/43 scale. Scott Schimpf

1949 Nash, USA model No. 3, 1/43 scale, 4-3/4-inch length. Scott Schimpf

Citroen 15, Solido, 1/43 scale, 4-3/8-inch length, made in France. Scott Schimpf

1948 Cadillac, Vitzsc, 1/43 scale, 5-1/8-inch length, made in Portugal. Scott Schimpf

1947 Chrysler Windsor, Vitzsc, 1/43 scale, 5-inch length, made in Portugal. Scott Schimpf

Volkswagen, Corgi, made in China. Scott Schimpf

1946 Chrysler Windsor, Solido, 1/43 scale, 5-inch length, made in France. Scott Schimpf

1949 Ford, Ertl, 4-3/4-inch length, made in China. Scott Schimpf

1958 Ford, 1/43 scale, made in England. Scott Schimpf

1950 Chevrolet, Solido, 1/43 scale, 4-1/2-inch length, made in France. Scott Schimpf

1955 Chevrolet sedan delivery, 1/43 scale, 4-3/4-inch length, USA model. Scott Schimpf

Model A Ford roadster, Nostalgic Miniatures, 3-1/8-inch length, made in USA. Scott Schimpf

1931 V-16 Cadillac, Solido, 1/43 scale, 5-1/8-inch length, made in France. Scott Schimpf

1957 Chevrolet, Corgi, 4-3/4-inch length, made in China. Scott Schimpf

1956 Ford replica, 6-inch length, made in China. Scott Schimpf

Road Champs scale model, Suburban Fire Chiefs, 1/43 scale, 5-1/4-inch length, made in China, offered with paint design and markings from Philadelphia, St. Louis, Hartford, Bowling Green and more.

1998 GMC Suburban, Code 3 Collectible, 1/64 scale, 3-1/4-inch length, with history and bevel mount.

(Left) 1950 Chevrolet panel truck, Mira, 9-1/2-inch length. Scott Schimpf

1950 Ford, Ertl, 7-1/2-inch length, Philadelphia Bureau of Fire. Scott Schimpf

1957 Chevrolet Bel Air, Corgi, 1/43 scale, 4-3/4-inch length. Scott Schimpf

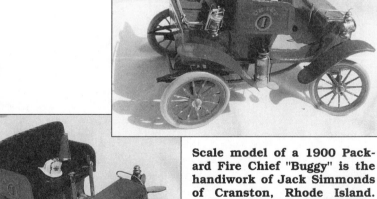

1934 Ford roadster, Jim Beam decanter, porcelain, 13-1/2-inch length. Beam also offered a Model A Ford Fire Chief car decanter.

Scale model of a 1900 Packard Fire Chief "Buggy" is the handiwork of Jack Simmonds of Cranston, Rhode Island. The model has incredible detail. From the front bench handrails to the oil lantern, it spells craftsmanship!

Pedal Cars & Rides for Playing "Chief"

The beginning of a professional fire fighter's career may have been motivated by family ties to the fire service. Many times, the power of suggestion will guide young minds to think positively in this direction. If the child plays and acts the role, and gets satisfaction and fun from play acting, the first link to a career will have been forged.

The toys of yesterday become the tools of today. Over one-third of the pedal cars sold have fire engine red or white paint and tiny ladders, or a bell, and lettering of the "Chief." These foot-powered 36 inches of pressed steel were pint-sized look-alikes to the real cars. A ten dollar bill would purchase one of these cars in 1935. Twenty dollars would buy a nice pressed steel Chief car around Christmastime in 1959. The bell was everything needed to put a smile on a child's face.

These pedal cars have also become collector items. The pictures on the following pages represent a few of the many makes available. All are from the pressed steel era. The last page is a brochure for the King Amusement Co., which manufactured a Kiddie Fire Chief Auto Ride.

AMF pedal car, 34-inch length, hubcaps missing.
Photo courtesy Karl Krouch

AMF pedal car (503), 34-inch length, hubcaps missing.
Photo courtesy Karl Krouch

Two AMF pedal cars from the 1960s. Both carry "Fire Chief" lettering. Photo courtesy Karl Krouch

Essex pedal car, 1934 model 506, 31-1/4-inch length, with bell and Pennsylvania license plate. Driver is author at three years of age. Photo courtesy Kenneth Peterson

1936 Ford pedal car, Garton, 1939 model, 35-inch length. Photos courtesy Ralph Harkins

1959 Plymouth pedal car, Murray, 1969 model with adjust-O-matic pedals, 36-inch length. Photo courtesy *Old Cars Weekly*

Pontiac Chief pedal car, Steelcraft model 535 DeLuxe (fenders, bumper), 38-inch length. Driver is Jim Stief of Upper Sandusky, Ohio. Photo courtesy Jack Paxton

BMC pedal car, 37-inch length, 1940s. Photo courtesy Karl Krouch

Murray pedal car, 1949 model F506, 33-1/2-inch length, $8.95 (1949). Photo courtesy Karl Krouch

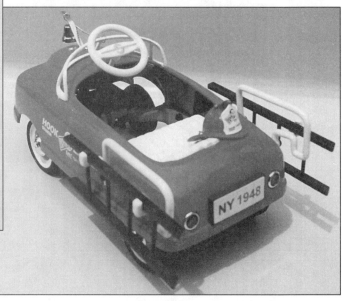

A miniature copy of the BMC pedal cars of the 1940s. This is a 1/6-scale model of the hook and ladder, which pedal car owners can't do without. Both pedals and steering are operable.

Kiddie Fire Chief Auto Ride

EIGHT BEAUTIFUL NEW FIRE CHIEF CARS

The Kiddie Fire Chief Auto Ride is soundly constructed and especially designed for portability. The ride can be set up easily by two men in one hour's time. Telescoped pipe standards are used and can be adjusted to set on the ground, wood floor, or cement walk; no foundations are necessary. The ride is extremely popular with children and has proven itself to be an excellent money maker requiring the very minimum of maintenance.

The Kiddie Fire Chief Auto Ride requires a space 20 ft. in diameter. Has eight beautiful new fire chief autos. These cars are exceptionally well built, have staunchly-constructed bodies and heavy duty steel frames. Bodies are moulded of modern high strength impregnated Fiberglas. Attractive moulded-in colors provide permanent beauty for the lifetime of the car. Each car comes complete with a bell and ladder. Wheels are heavy duty industrial type, size 2x10, with ball bearings and zerk grease fittings. Size of the car over-all is 51 inches long, 22 inches high, and 23 inches wide. Each car has ample room for two children. Ride comes complete with 1½ H. P. electric motor and automatic clutch for gentle starting.

We also include a 50 ft. lead cable, switch boxes, and fluorescent fixtures for lighting. The floor sections are kiln-dried fir and metal bound. The crestings and medallions are white pine with masonite trim. We furnish exceptionally good shipping crates that are built so that each piece can slip into its own compartment. Electrical equipment has been inspected by the City of Detroit, and the safety engineers have given the ride sand bag tests and fully approved of the mechanical features.

Fire Chief Autos can be purchased separately. Modernize your old Auto Ride with a set of these beautiful new cars.

KING AMUSEMENT COMPANY

82 ORCHARD STREET   **MOUNT CLEMENS, MICHIGAN, U. S. A.**

Convenient Terms Can Be Arranged on All Riding Devices

All Prices Quoted Are F. O. B. Mt. Clemens, Mich.,

Shipping Weight 4000 lbs.

CHIEF'S CARS EXCERPTS

To supplement the book's photographic history of Chief cars, excerpts from the National Board of Fire Underwriters field reports on "Chief's Cars" comprise this section.

The Underwriters board was established in the 19th century, and did more to help in the field of fire prevention than any other single organization. In the early days of the 20th century the Underwriters were busy inspecting city fire fighting facilities and making recommendations.

Teams of Engineers compiled reports of uniform information on three topics: City in General, Fire Fighting Facilities, and Structural Conditions and Hazards. These topics were divided into subtopics, and subdivided again into paragraphs of valuable information. One of these paragraphs always related to the "Chief's cars," under Fire Department Equipment. Hundreds of city reports were researched for this particular paragraph, and reviewed for content and connective interest as an excerpt.

The early excerpts define the number of Chief buggies and wagons in service and also in reserve. Later reports indicate the automobiles in service, sometimes by make, body style, and age, and give interesting details of the automobiles' fire fighting equipment. Subsequent reports include radio equipment installed. Comments on the automobiles' condition and use factors were common.

The excerpts listed were selected for both reading enjoyment and to further understanding of the cities' progression of automobiles used by the fire departments of our nation.

All information is listed alphabetically by city and state, followed in order by the date of each report.

Akron, OH	1912	The chief is provided with an automobile equipped with a 25 gallon chemical tank, 150 feet of chemical hose, 3 portable chemical extinguishers, and a motor-generator set to furnish current for electric head lights and a portable searchlight. It also carries other minor equipment and two firemen.
Akron, OH	1927	The chief and the assistant chief on duty are each provided with a high speed automobile. The assistant chief's car carries 3 chemical extinguishers, wrecking bar, Burrell smoke masks, and a surgical kit; the assistant chief's car had a 25 gallon chemical tank with 150 feet of chemical hose, ax, surgical kit, 3 chemical extinguishers, gas key, spanners, and wrenches; each carries a portable telephone set for communicating with headquarters. An extra driver and 2 men accompany the assistant chief's car.
Albany, GA	1955	A 1953 Buick, 4-door sedan, equipped with radio, is provided for the chief; the two assistant chiefs are provided with a 1948 Chevrolet coupe and a 1947 Chevrolet pickup truck.
Albany, NY	1912	Improvements authorized an automobile for the chief. Three chief wagons in service, one in reserve.
Albany, NY	1949	A Buick sedan is provided for the chief and a Buick 2 door sedan and two Packard coupes for the battalion chiefs. None are equipped with radio. An old touring car is in reserve and another Packard coupe is used by the master mechanic.
Albuquerque, NM	1949	A 1947 convertible, equipped with a 3-way radio, is provided for the use of the chief officers; assistant chiefs use their private automobiles when the department car is not available.
Albuquerque, NM	1958	The chief is provided with a 1957 Dodge convertible, the assistant chiefs on duty with a 1955 Ford and a 1957 Chevrolet 4-door sedan, and the fire prevention bureau with a 1957 Ford 4-door sedan.
Alexandria, LA	1927	The chief is provided with a 4-cylinder Nash runabout equipped with wire cutters, double male and female connection and rubber gloves.
Alexandria, LA	1955	A 1954 Buick sedan, equipped with 3-way radio, is provided for the use of the chief or the assistant chief.
Alhambra, CA	1952	A 1949 Pontiac sedan serves as chief's car and a 1949 Pontiac coupe as assistant chief's car. Both are radio equipped and the assistant chief's car carried a smoke ejector, gas mask, life line and rubber gloves. A 1948 Buick radio-equipped ambulance is at Station 2 and a 1939 Ford pickup truck is used as a utility wagon.
Alton, IL	1948	A 1940 Hudson sedan is provided for use of the chief.
Alton, IL	1958	The assistant chief on duty is provided with a 1956 Chevrolet sedan; the chief uses his private car for business. The chief's car is equipped with a 3-way radio unit on the police department system.
Altoona, PA	1908	Chief's wagon, 1 in service.
Anaheim, CA	1958	Two 1957 Ford 4-door sedans are provided for the chief and assistant chief, a 1955 Ford sedan for the battalion chief on duty and a 1957 Ford station wagon for the fire marshal. A 1949 Plymouth 4-door sedan is in reserve and a 1955 Studebaker pickup truck is used by the hydrant inspector. All stations, fire apparatus, department cars and the truck are equipped with a 3-way FM radio.
Anderson, IN	1929	The chief is provided with a Buick coupe, purchased in 1928.
Appleton, WI	1931	The chief is provided with a 1926 Reo sport roadster.
Arlington, MA	1950	1948 and 1946 Oldsmobile 4-door sedans are provided for the chief and deputy chief respectively; each is equipped with two-way radio and carries an all-service gas mask and a dry-powder extinguisher.
Asbury Park, NJ	1958	The chief is provided with a 1957 Chevrolet 4-door sedan and the deputy chiefs with a 1957 Chevrolet station wagon.
Asheville, NC	1953	The chief is provided with a 1949 Pontiac sedan and the assistant chief on duty with a 1948 Pontiac sedan; both cars are 3 way radio equipped. Each car is equipped with two knapsack type pump tanks, a first aid kit and a few minor tools.

Ashland, KY	1925	The chief is provided with a Haynes roadster equipped with a 30-gallon chemical tank and 150 feet of 3/4-inch hose. Apparatus tanks are filled as needed from a tank wagon.
Ashland, KY	1945	The chief is provided with a late model Dodge coupe. Gasoline would be transported to extended fires in the chief's car, using a five-gallon safety can.
Atchison, KS	1912	Recommendations of Underwriters - That the service be improved: by providing an automobile for the chief.
Athens, GA	1954	A 1948 Buick 4-door sedan, 3-way radio equipped, is provided for the chief. When he is off duty, it is kept at fire headquarters and would be dispatched to his home in event the chief was needed at the scene of a fire; the assistant chief on duty normally responds on Engine 1.
Atlanta, GA	1914	The chief and two assistant chiefs respond to first alarms in the congested value and adjoining districts, and to second alarms elsewhere. The assistant chiefs are not provided with buggies, and have to respond with the apparatus in their headquarters. A general alarm calls out the entire department. Chief's Wagons, 1 in service, 1 in reserve.
Atlanta, GA	1954	The chief and assistant chief on duty are each provided with a 1950 Oldsmobile sedan and the two battalion chiefs on duty have a 1951 Buick and 1951 Oldsmobile. A 1952 Chevrolet sedan is provided for the arson investigator, and a 1937 LaSalle sedan is assigned to the Superintendent of Repairs; a 1948 Oldsmobile sedan is used as a spare chief's car. All automobiles are radio equipped.
Atlantic City, NJ	1952	Five sedans, purchased between 1946 and 1950, are provided for the chief officers and fire marshal; one spare sedan is provided.
Augusta, GA	1905	The chief has one rubber-tired wagon in service and one in reserve.
Augusta, GA	1940	A 1939 Cadillac sedan is provided for the use of the chief, and a 1940 Chevrolet sedan is provided for the assistant chief on duty.
Augusta, GA	1952	A 1950 Buick sedan is provided for use of the chief and two 1950 Mercury sedans are provided for the assistant and battalion chiefs on duty. All are three-way radio equipped and in good condition. The chief inspector is provided with a 1947 Oldsmobile which is in poor condition.
Augusta, ME	1907	Privately owned, Chief wagon, 1 in service
Aurora, IL	1922	The chief is provided with a Reo roadster carrying hand extinguishers and an electric lantern.
Aurora, IL	1937	The chief is provided with a 1931 Studebaker 8-cylinder coupe.
Bangor, ME	1907	Wagons, chiefs wagons, 1 in service.
Bangor, ME	1927	A 7-passenger Cadillac touring car is used as squad car. The chief is provided with a 2-passenger Studebaker roadster.
Bangor, ME	1955	The chief is provided with a 1953 Buick 4-door sedan, equipped with a 3-way police radio unit; the deputy chief has no car but rides one of the pieces of apparatus in headquarters except at night and at other times when the chief is not on duty and leaves the car at headquarters.
Barberton, OH	1950	The chief is provided with a 1942 Chevrolet coach equipped with a three-way radio tuned to police radio frequency.
Bartlesville, OK	1959	The city does not provide either chief officer with a car, but grants both officers an allowance for using their personal cars for fire department business.
Bay City, MI	1911	Wagons, Chief's, 2 in service.
Bay City, MI	1930	The chief is provided with a Buick roadster purchased in 1925.
Belleville, IL	1920	The chief is provided with a Studebaker runabout, purchased in 1916, equipped with a 30-gallon chemical tank, 200 feet of chemical hose, and a smoke helmet.
Belleville, IL	1926	The chief is provided with a Studebaker runabout purchased in 1925. It carries one 2-1/2-gallon chemical extinguisher, one 2-1/2-gallon hand pump, one ax, and a smoke helmet.
Belleville, IL	1938	The chief is provided with a Buick sedan purchased in 1936. It carries a chemical extinguisher, rope ladder, rope gun, hydrant wrench, smoke mask, and spanners.
Bellingham, WA	1920	One small automobile is provided for the use of the chiefs, equipped with a 20-gallon chemical tank and 200 feet of 1/2-inch hose.
Berkeley, CA	1910	The chief is provided with an automobile, and the battalion chiefs have horse-drawn buggies. Supply and hay wagons are kept at Ladder 1 with the extra horses.
Berkeley, CA	1951	Late model sedans are provided for the chief, deputy chief and the two assistant chiefs on duty. Each carries a filter type gas mask, 2-quart pressure type carbon-tetrachloride extinguisher and is equipped with 3-way FM radio; the chiefs' car also carries a portable loud speaker. Three 1951 Ford coupes are provided for fire prevention inspectors.
Berlin, NH	1925	Pungs or runners are provided for each company for winter use. No car is provided for the chief; he uses his own automobile to some extent, although receiving nothing from the city toward its maintenance operation.
Bernardino, CA	1936	Allowance is made by the city for the use of private cars of the chief and inspector.
Bernardino, CA		1947A sedan and pickup truck, both equipped with 2-way radio, are furnished for use of chief officers and a light coupe for utility purposes. The chief and first assistant chief use their private cars when responding from their residences at night.
Berwyn, IL	1932	The chief is provided with a 1928 Chevrolet roadster.
Bessemer, AL	1939	The chief and the assistant chief use their private cars for fire department operations. Each is equipped with a radio receiving set. The city supplies them with gasoline and oil.
Bethlehem, PA	1950	A 1947 Dodge coupe and a 1938 Buick coupe are provided for use of the chief and one assistant chief; one assistant chief provides his own transportation.

Beverly Hills, CA	1939	A 1937 model coupe furnished for the chief is equipped with 2-way radio and carries a 35-gallon water tank, booster pump, 50 feet of garden hose, and a small amount of other equipment. The chief's car has a magnetic device for operating street traffic signals in connection with sensitive relays located under street pavements.
Billings, MT	1945	A Ford coupe of 1941 model is provided for use of the chief. The aerial ladder truck is used in lieu of a utility truck.
Biloxi, MS	1953	The chief is provided with a 1951 Plymouth 2-door sedan, which is left at headquarters at night for the assistant chief to use, but the assistant chiefs seldom use the car to respond to fires, riding the ladder truck instead. There is no minor equipment carried in the chief's car.
Binghamton, NY	1916	The chief and first assistant chief are each provided with a 5 passenger automobile; the car assigned to the first assistant chief is used for the most part by the acting fire marshal.
Binghamton, NY	1954	Three chief cars in service. The chief is provided with a 1946 Buick 4 door sedan; when he is off duty the car is kept at headquarters and in the event of an alarm to which he would respond, his driver would proceed to his home. A 1951 DeSoto 4 door station wagon is in service at headquarters for use by the assistant chief on duty. It is equipped with a small amount of minor equipment including two self contained breathing apparatus. A 1947 Ford 4 door sedan is provided for the battalion chief on duty at station #2. All chief cars are 3 way radio equipped. The fire prevention bureau is assigned a 1949 Chevrolet 4 door sedan, radio equipped.
Birmingham, AL	1909	1 car and 2 wagons in service.
Birmingham, AL	1923	Three Cadillac touring cars, 1 Cadillac roadster and 1 Stephens car are used by the chief officers. All are in good condition; the chief's car has a motor siren. The chief carries an army type gas mask.
Birmingham, AL	1939	Seven automobiles are provided for use by the chief officers and drill masters; 3 cars carry some minor equipment which includes 4 to 6 salvage covers, gas mask, tannic acid kit and extra sprinkler heads. The chief's automobile is equipped with a radio receiver. A sedan automobile, located at Station 12, is equipped with 3 water drums of 55 gallons capacity each, a 165 gallon capacity pump and 200 feet of 3/4-inch hose; it is used for grass fires.
Bloomfield, NJ	1939	The chief officer on duty is provided with a Buick sedan which is equipped with a radio receiver tuned to the police broadcast system.
Bloomington, IL	1927	The chief is provided with a Hupmobile roadster.
Bloomington, IL	1943	The marshal is provided with a 4-year-old Pontiac coupe. A 16-year-old Cadillac chassis, with a hose body, a 3-way mounted turret, two inhalators, and three filter-type masks and one oxygen mask, is operated to rescue calls and to other special alarms. A 17-year-old truck, carrying a Kohler 2,400-watt generator and two mounted and four portable floodlights, responds to extended night fires.
Boise, ID	1922	The chief is provided with a 2-passenger Buick roadster.
Boise, ID	1931	A Willys-Knight cabriolet is furnished for the chief.
Boise, ID	1945	A Nash coupe of 1939 model is furnished for use of the chief.
Boise, ID	1952	The chief is provided with a 1951 Ford sedan, equipped with 3-way radio.
Boston, MA	1925	Automobiles are provided for the commissioner, chief and assistant chief, heads of departments, medical examiner and each deputy and district chief on duty, with a good reserve supply. Other automobiles include 2 Chief cars. There are also several hose and ladder pungs, and sleighs and chief's buggies for salting hydrants. Chief's Automobiles, 31 in service, 13 in reserve, and Chiefs' Wagons, 2 in reserve.
Bridgeport, CT	1912	The chief is provided with an automobile fitted with a 35-gallon pressure chemical tank and a searchlight. The first assistant chief is provided with an automobile and second assistant chief has a horse and buggy.
Bridgeport, CT	1944	A 1942 Chrysler sedan, equipped with a two-way radio, is provided for the chief. Two Dodge sedans are provided for the assistant chiefs on duty and two coupes for the use of the superintendent of fire alarm.
Bridgeport, CT	1954	The chief and each assistant chief on duty are provided 4-door Chrysler sedans purchased in 1951, 1952 or 1953. The superintendent of fire alarm has a 1949 Studebaker sedan, the inspector of combustibles a 1950 Ford sedan, and the master mechanic a 1949 Ford coupe; all of these vehicles are 3-way radio equipped.
Bristol, CT	1958	A 1953 Oldsmobile sedan and a 1956 Mercury station wagon are provided for the chief and deputy chiefs, respectively.
Brockton, MA	1908	Wagons, Chief's 2 in service, 1 in reserve
Brockton, MA	1958	The chief is provided with a 1956 Cadillac 4-door sedan and the deputy chiefs share the use of a 1954 Pontiac 4-door sedan; the latter vehicle carries a small amount of minor equipment. The fire prevention bureau has a 1957 Plymouth 4-door sedan.
Buffalo, NY	1916	The chief has a five passenger automobile; the assistant chief, each battalion chief, the master mechanic, the superintendent of horses and chief operator of the fire alarm system have a runabout. Four chief's wagons, 6 chief's sleighs are in reserve.
Buffalo, NY	1927	Thirteen chief automobiles are in service; two in reserve.
Buffalo, NY	1952	The commissioner has a 1950 Buick sedan and the deputy commissioners, battalion chiefs and chief of training have a 1948, 1949, or 1950 Chevrolet 2 door sedan; all are equipped with radio. A 1948 Chevrolet sedan is used by the members of the airport company. A 1950 Chevrolet sedan is provided as a spare car for the commissioner and two 1947 and one 1948 Chevrolet 2 door sedans are in reserve, all equipped with radio.
Burlington, IA	1929	The chief is provided with a Dodge roadster, purchased in 1926, equipped with two hand chemical extinguishers.
Burlington, IA	1955	The chief is provided with a 1949 Buick sedan.
Burlington, VT	1907	Chief's wagons, 1 in service.

Burlington, VT	1954	A 1950 Oldsmobile four-door sedan is furnished for the chief. A 1950 GMC 1-ton pickup truck, known as Car 12, carrying hose and minor equipment, including an inhalator and a smoke ejector, is provided for the deputy chief and his driver; it is radio-equipped and in addition, carries a walkie-talkie unit.
Butte, MT	1910	The chief is supplied with a horse and buggy.
Butte, MT	1930	A Packard roadster of 1927 model with chemical tank and oxygen masks, used as a squad car is in service at headquarters.
Butte, MT	1937	A Packard roadster of 1927 model with chemical tank and oxygen masks, used as a squad car, is in service at headquarters.
Camden, NJ	1923	Four Buick roadsters are provided for the use of the chief, each deputy chief and the battalion chief on duty; the deputy chief's car not in use is used as a reserve car.
Camden, NJ	1950	A 1948 and a 1949 Buick 2-door sedans and two 1937 Chevrolet coupes are provided for chief officers; each carries a one-gallon carbon tetrachloride extinguisher, one or two type N gas masks, and a few other pieces of minor equipment and the deputy chief's car also has two self-contained breathing apparatus and a portable iron lung. None of the automobiles are equipped with radio. Headquarters and Station 3 each have a rowboat with trailer; trailer attachment is provided on the chiefs' automobiles.
Canton, OH	1912	The chief has a rubber-tired buggy.
Canton, OH	1921	The chief has a 7-passenger automobile. A 1912 4 cylinder touring car, equipped as a supply wagon, is used by the assistant chief.
Canton, OH	1950	A 1947, four-door sedan is provided for use of the chief, and two recent model two-door sedans for the assistant chief. All are equipped with three-way radios, tuned to police radio frequency. A driver is detailed to the chief's car, but no drivers are assigned to the assistant chief's car. The chief is on continuous duty, responding from his office during the day and from his residence during the night.
Cedar Rapids, IA	1915	The chief owns a 30-horsepower 5-passenger Chandler automobile in which he attends fires.
Charleston, SC	1906	The chief uses an automobile which carries two 3-gallon extinguishers and an ax. One chief's wagon is in reserve.
Charleston, SC	1950	A 1948 two-door sedan, a 1946 four-door sedan and a 1946 coupe, all Chevrolets, are provided for the use of the chief, assistant chiefs and battalion chiefs, respectively. Each have a radio receiver and the assistant and battalion chiefs' cars carry a self-contained breathing apparatus or an all-purpose gas mask.
Charleston, WV	1914	This is a 2-passenger runabout automobile carrying a 35-gallon Kanawha compressed air chemical tank. Two of the four men who respond with it ride on the steps. There is a chief's buggy belonging to the fire department, which is regularly used by the police department.
Charleston, WV	1935	The chief is provided with a Chevrolet coupe; the assistant chief rides the apparatus.
Charleston, WV	1954	A 1953 DeSoto 4-door sedan is provided for the chief and a 1952 Chevrolet 4-door sedan is assigned to the Fire Prevention Bureau.
Charlotte, NC	1923	The chief is provided with an Essex roadster. A Ford roadster, with a truck body, is also provided for fire alarm and general utility use.
Charlotte, NC	1940	The chief and the assistant chief on duty each has a 5 passenger car equipped with a 2 way radio.
Chattanooga, TN	1948	Three 1947 Ford coupes or sedans, all equipped with 2-way radios tuned to police radio frequency, are provided for use of the police officers, but no chief's drivers are assigned.
Chattanooga, TN	1955	The chief, assistant chiefs, drillmaster, fire marshal and assistant fire marshals are provided with Ford and Chevrolet 2-door sedans. Few tools and no extinguishers are carried.
Chelsea, MA	1920	The chief is provided with a 6-cylinder Hudson automobile equipped with a 35-gallon chemical tank, 300 feet of 3/4-inch hose and 250 feet of 2-inch linen hose with 2-1/2-inch couplings. This car responds to all alarms and carries two men besides the chief, who act as an auxiliary squad.
Chelsea, MA	1959	The chief is provided with a 1950 Packard 4-door sedan in only fairly good condition, and the deputy chief on duty uses a 1954 Ford 4-door sedan; one of the deputy chiefs, when on duty, shares the use of the chief's car and aide.
Chester, PA	1914	The city furnishes a buggy and a set of harnesses for the chief, but no horse. If the chief does not own a horse he uses the street cars. The present chief has an automobile, and the chief's buggy is used by the second assistant chief, who owns a horse.
Chester, PA	1955	Three radio-equipped 2-door sedans, a 1954 Ford and two 1953 Chevrolets, are provided for use by the chief officers; each carries a carbon dioxide extinguisher and one filter-type gas mask.
Chillicothe, OH	1948	The chief is provided with a 1947 Chevrolet sedan, equipped with a 1-way radio, siren, and red lights.
Cincinnati, OH	1915	The chief, marshals, assistant marshals, mechanical engineer and superintendent of fire alarm are each provided with an automobile; 4 chief's buggies are in reserve. Marshals' cars for districts 3 and 4 each have a 40 gallon chemical tank with 2-1/2 inch hose connections, 200 or 500 feet of 1 inch chemical hose, ax, extra chemical charge and 2 lanterns.
Cincinnati, OH	1943	The chief is provided with a new sedan. Fourteen coupes are used by the chief officers, marshals and bureau heads with three available for replacements.
Cincinnati, OH	1957	The chief, assistant chiefs, drillmaster and marshals are provided with late model, 2 or 4 door Chevrolet sedans and the two supervisors are provided with 1949 Ford sedans. Five automobiles are in reserve.
Clarksburg, WV	1925	A Chevrolet 6-cylinder roadster is provided for the chief; the assistant chiefs ride with their respective shift on the headquarter's apparatus.
Clarksburg, WV	1928	The chief is provided with a 4-cylinder 1928 Whippet roadster. The assistant chiefs ride with the headquarters shift on the apparatus.
Cleveland Heights, OH	1957	The chief is provided with a 1953 Pontiac 4-door sedan, the assistant chiefs a 1954 Ford 2-door sedan. The two cars used by the chiefs carry a small amount of minor equipment.
Cleveland, OH	1912	Chief's automobile, 4 in service; Chief's wagons, 11 in service, 1 in reserve.

Cleveland, OH	1925	The chief has a 7 passenger White automobile over 10 years old, and of a discontinued make. The first assistant chief has a Cadillac roadster and the second assistant chief drives a White roadster over 11 years old, which the first assistant chief discarded. Battalion chiefs drive Ford roadsters.
Cleveland, OH	1931	The chief has a new 7 passenger sedan. The assistant chiefs have Peerless roadsters and the battalion chiefs have Ford roadsters or coupes. Part of these cars are equipped with radio receiving sets tuned to the police broadcasting station. 17 cars in service, 6 cars in reserve.
Cleveland, OH	1955	There are 13 sedans provided for the fire-fighting force, including a 1948 Chrysler for the chief, a car for each assistant chief and each battalion chief on duty. In addition there are 26 other sedans for the use of various bureaus and individuals in the department. Battalion chief's cars carry a dry-powder extinguisher, a small gated wye, distributing nozzle, 2 filter-type gas masks, hand light and a hydrant wrench. There are four chief's cars in reserve. Most sedans are of Chevrolet or Ford make purchased between 1944 and 1952 and some are in only fair condition.
Clifton, NJ	1956	The chief and assistant chief on duty are provided with a 1954 and 1953 Pontiac sedan.
Clinton, IA	1928	The chief is provided with a 1928 model 5-passenger Buick touring car.
Clinton, IA	1946	The chief is provided with a 1939 Packard sedan which carries a Type N gas mask and two-quart vaporizing liquid type extinguisher.
Columbia, SC	1907	Chief's wagons, 1 in service.
Columbia, SC	1938	The chief is provided with a 5-passenger 1936 Buick carrying 2 hand extinguishers, first-aid kit, gas key, smoke mask and 2 hydrant wrenches.
Columbia, SC	1951	A 1949 Lincoln, a 1949 Studebaker and a 1948 Studebaker are provided for the use of the chief, assistant-chief and chief of the Bureau of Fire Prevention, respectively. All are equipped with 3-way radio. The chief's and assistant-chief's car carry one or two approved filter-type gas masks, 2 or 3 small extinguishers and a first-aid kit and each has a 3-way hand radio set.
Columbus, GA	1930	The chief is provided with a 1929 Buick coupe; the assistant chiefs ride on the fire apparatus.
Columbus, GA	1940	The chief is provided with a 1936 Studebaker coupe equipped with a radio receiver tuned to the police broadcasting station.
Columbus, GA	1953	A 1950 Ford 4-door sedan and 1947 Mercury 4-door sedan are provided for the chief and assistant chief, respectively; both cars are 3-way radio equipped. A government surplus Willys Jeep is provided for use by the master mechanic.
Columbus, OH	1954	The chief, deputy chief, assistant chiefs, and battalion chiefs are provided with late model sedans. Other automobiles are provided for use of the communications division, training department, fire prevention bureau, shop, and squad captain; three cars are in reserve, 18 in service.
Compton, CA	1953	Additional fire department vehicles include a 1946 Dodge coupe for the chief, a 1950 Ford coupe for the battalion chiefs, a 1949 Ford coupe for fire prevention bureau and a 1951 Chevrolet 1/2-ton pickup truck used as a utility truck. The three automobiles are radio-equipped.
Concord, NH	1950	A 1948 and a 1946 Buick sedans are provided for the chief and deputy chief respectively, cars are 2-way-radio equipped.
Coral Gables, FL	1957	Two 1954 Ford 4-door sedans, both radio equipped, are provided, one for use by the chief and the other shared by the assistant chief and fire prevention inspector.
Council Bluffs, IA	1927	A 2-passenger automobile carrying one respirator, two 2-1/2-gallon soda-acid and one carbon tetra-chloride extinguishers is provided for the chief. The car is 14 years old. It is also used as a supply car when needed, a 5-gallon open can being used to deliver gasoline to fires.
Covington, KY	1911	Chief's wagon, 1 in service.
Covington, KY	1922	The chief is provided with a Stutz roadster which carries a 2-1/2-gallon chemical extinguisher and electric hand lanterns.
Covington, KY	1952	The chief is provided with a 1941 Oldsmobile coupe, and the assistant chiefs share a car which is identical with the chief's. Both are provided with 3-way radio, gas masks and portable extinguishers. A self-contained breathing apparatus is carried in the assistant chief's car.
Daly City, CA	1958	A 1951 Ford coupe is assigned to the chief. A 1947 Chevrolet pickup truck, acquired second-hand, is assigned to a battalion chief whenever it is not in use for fire prevention, fire alarm maintenance or general utility work.
Danville, IL	1947	The chief is provided with a coupe. A 1925 Lincoln passenger car, rebuilt as an ambulance, carrying two inhalators, blankets, stretcher, and other rescue and life-saving equipment, is kept at headquarters station and is manned by firemen when needed.
Danville, VA	1921	A Ford runabout is provided for the use of the chief.
Danville, VA	1930	The chief is provided with a Buick roadster. The assistant chief responds to alarms on Engine 1.
Danville, VA	1951	A 1942 Buick 2-door sedan and a 1941 Ford coupe, both equipped with 2-way radio tuned to the police radio system, are in use by the chief and assistant chief, respectively.
Davenport, IA	1909	The chief and first assistant have rubber-tired buggies in service.
Davenport, IA	1930	The chief is provided with a 7-passenger Marmon touring car, purchased in 1922. Two Ford cars, purchased about 1915, are kept at headquarters. One is equipped with a chemical tank. The other carries a small truck body and is utilized for general work.
Dayton, OH	1914	The chief and three marshals have each a rubber-tired buggy.
Dayton, OH	1958	Three 1957 Ford 4-door sedans are provided for the chief and 2 assistant chiefs. The district chiefs are provided with nine 1954 to 1956 Chevrolet or Ford 4-door sedans, and six 1951 to 1956 Chevrolet sedans are assigned to various activities.
Daytona Beach, FL	1953	A 1946 Dodge 4-door sedan is provided for the chief; it is radio equipped operating on the police department frequency. No vehicle is provided for the assistant chief on duty.

Dearborn, MI	1930	The chief is provided with a Lincoln roadster equipped with a smoke mask, inhalator and first-aid kit. A Ford roadster is in reserve.
Decatur, AL	1957	A 1955 Ford sedan and a 1956 Chevrolet sedan are provided for the use of the chief and assistant, respectively. The assistant chief's automobile is equipped with a public address system and one is to be installed in the chief's car in the near future.
Decatur, IL	1915	The chief is provided with a four-passenger, 40 horse-power Rambler automobile and the assistant chief has a rubber tired buggy, which he used in going to meals and for inspection work.
Decatur, IL	1923	The chief is provided with a Chalmers touring car; bids were opened in June, 1923, for a new chief's car. The assistant chief, who is on duty alternate days, responds to fires with the service or aerial truck.
Decatur, IL	1938	The chief is provided with a 2-way radio-equipped 1937 Dodge sedan.
Decatur, IL	1947	The chief is provided with a 1942, Buick coach equipped with a 2-way radio.
Denver, CO	1910	The chief and one assistant chief are provided with 4-cylinder gasoline motor cars. Each of the other assistant chiefs has two horses and a rubber tired buggy.
Denver, CO	1939	Fifteen closed cars are provided for the chief officers, other responsible officers and the inspectors.
Des Moines, IA	1915	The chief is provided with a Chalmers 38-horsepower, 2-passenger automobile, the first assistant chief with a Chalmers 40-horsepower, 5-passenger automobile and the second assistant chief with a rubber-tired buggy.
Dubuque, IA	1909	The chief has a buggy at headquarters.
Dubuque, IA	1925	The chief is provided with a seven-passenger Cadillac automobile.
Dubuque, IA	1931	A Packard 5-passenger sedan is provided for the use of the chief.
Dubuque, IA	1947	A 1938 Studebaker sedan is provided for the use of the chief; it is equipped with two-way radio and also carries two self-contained breathing units and one Type N gas mask.
Duluth, MN	1908	Chief's wagons, 3 in service, 1 in reserve., Chief's sleighs, 3 in reserve.
Durham, NC	1925	The chief is provided with a 5 passenger automobile. The assistant chief responds on the pumper.
Durham, NC	1955	The chief is provided with a 1954 Buick, the assistant and deputy chief on duty each with a 1948 Buick, and the fire inspector with a 1946 Ford, all are 4 door sedans equipped with 3 way radios.
E. Chicago, IN	1938	The chief is provided with a 1936 Ford V-8 coupe.
E. Chicago, IN	1954	A 1953 and a 1951 Ford sedan are provided for the chief and the assistant chiefs, respectively; each is equipped with a filter-type gas mask and 3-way radio.
E. Cleveland, OH	1926	The chief is provided with a Ford runabout, equipped with a Burrell smoke mask. Car is in poor condition.
E. Hartford, CT	1955	The chief is provided with a 1950 Pontiac 4-door sedan, the assistant chief with a 1954 Ford sedan and the fire marshal with a 1951 Ford sedan; none of these cars is radio-equipped.
E. Orange, NJ	1914	The chief is provided with a rubber-tired buggy.
E. Orange, NJ	1952	A 1947 and a 1942 Buick sedan, both equipped with 2-way fire department radio, are provided for use of chief officers on duty.
E. Providence, RI	1950	A 1949 Oldsmobile sedan and a 1947 Chevrolet sedan are provided for the chief and deputy chief respectively. Both of these cars are 2-way radio equipped and carry a small amount of minor equipment.
E. St. Louis, IL	1929	A Dodge roadster, purchased in 1927, is utilized by the assistant chiefs. The chief's car was recently wrecked and has not been replaced at this date.
East Liverpool, OH	1927	The chief is provided with an Oldsmobile roadster, which has been in an unserviceable condition for the past year.
East Liverpool, OH	1950	The chief is provided with a 1949 Chevrolet sedan.
Eastchester, NY	1951	A 1950 Chevrolet coupe and a 1942 Buick sedan are provided for chief officers use. The Chevrolet carries an inhalator and a foam aspirating nozzle.
Easton, PA	1915	A rubber-tired buggy is provided for the chief; it carries emergency supplies and tools for repair work on the fire alarm system and is used by the lineman.
Easton, PA	1941	The chief is provided with a 1927 Packard roadster which is in good condition.
Easton, PA	1955	A 1946 Chevrolet business coupe is provided for the chief. It carries 1 self-contained breathing apparatus and 2 filter-type masks and a small amount of minor equipment.
Eau Claire, WI	1935	The chief is provided with a 1929 Reo coupe.
Eau Claire, WI	1952	The chief is provided with a 5-passenger, 1948 Nash coupe with two-way radio. The assistant chief uses either the chief's car or responds to fires with Engine 2.
Elgin, IL	1923	The chief is provided with a 6-cylinder Nash roadster.
Elgin, IL	1928	The chief is provided with a 6-cylinder Hupmobile roadster equipped with one Pyrene extinguisher and a Burrell all-service gas mask.
Elgin, IL	1932	The chief is provided with a 6-cylinder Buick sedan equipped with one Pyrene extinguisher and an all-service gas mask.
Elgin, IL	1957	A 1950 Buick 4-door sedan is provided for the chief.
Elizabeth, NJ	1916	The chief and deputy chief are each provided with a 50-horsepower, 4-passenger Apperson automobile, with a Buick 5-passenger automobile in reserve; the latter is being overhauled in the shop.
Elkhart, IN	1949	The chief is provided with a 1948 Buick sedan equipped with two-way radio. Assistant chiefs respond on apparatus.
Erie, PA	1915	The city provides a horse and buggy for the chief and assistant chief.
Eugene, OR	1938	The chief uses his personal car to drive to fires.
Evanston, IL	1930	The chief is provided with a 1926 model Lincoln 7-passenger touring car, in which is carried a smoke mask and a first-aid kit.

Fairmont, WV	1950	The chief is provided with a 1946 Dodge sedan, which also has 2-way radio; the assistant chief uses his personal automobile.
Fall River, MA	1948	The chief, assistant chief and the district chief on duty are provided with 2-way radio-equipped 1948 Buick automobiles; appliances carried include a resuscitator, all-service gas mask, salvage covers, electric hand light and first-aid kit.
Fargo, ND	1928	A 2 passenger car equipped with a small truck body is used by the chief.
Fargo, ND	1951	A sedan equipped with 2 way radio is provided for use of the chief.
Fayetteville, NC	1953	A 1951 Hudson 4 door sedan and a 1951 Plymouth 4 door sedan are provided for the chief and the assistant chiefs.
Fayetteville, NC	1958	A 1955 Pontiac and a 1955 Ford sedans have been provided for the chief officers.
Ferndale, MI	1953	The chief is provided with a 1949 Ford coupe.
Fitchburg, MA	1917	The chief is provided with an 8-cylinder, 7 passenger Cadillac automobile purchased in 1915; it carries two 3-gallon extinguishers and an ax. A spare chief's buggy and wagon are provided. The chief is provided with a light pung.
Flint, MI	1950	Seven automobiles are provided for use of the chief officers and inspectors. Chief officers' cars are equipped with two-way radios; battalion chiefs' cars each carry a Type "N" gas mask and a self-contained breathing apparatus, an inhalator or resuscitator, first-aid kit, life line, one or two waterproof covers and spare sprinkler heads.
Florence, AL	1957	A 1947 Chrysler sedan is provided for use by the chief and is equipped with 3-way radio; it is to be replaced with a new Ford sedan within a short time. No car is provided for the assistant chief on duty.
Fond Du Lac, WI	1933	The chief is provided with a 1929 Buick 6-cylinder sedan.
Fond Du Lac, WI	1953	A 1949 Ford sedan is provided for the use of the chief officers; it is equipped with a two-way radio and with some minor first-aid appliances.
Fort Dodge, IA	1929	The chief is provided with a Chrysler touring car purchased in 1925.
Fort Dodge, IA	1954	A 1952 Oldsmobile sedan is provided for the use of the chief. It carries a filter-type gas mask.
Fort Smith, AR	1932	Two 1932 Dodge, 8-cylinder closed cars are provided for the chief officers. Equipment, consisting of oxygen helmets, gas masks, first-aid kits, gas keys, water keys, wire cutters, wrenches, sprinkler kits and lanterns has been ordered.
Freeport, IL	1909	Chief's wagon, privately owned, 1 in service.
Freeport, IL	1926	The chief is provided with a dilapidated, second-hand, 2-passenger Ford car carrying 2 hand extinguishers.
Fresno, CA	1911	Chief's motorcycles, 2 in service.
Fresno, CA	1945	A sedan with 2-way radio is furnished for the chief, a coupe with 2-way radio for the platoon chief on duty and 3 coupes with radio receivers for assistant chiefs and master mechanic.
Ft. Lauderdale, FL	1953	The chief is provided with a Studebaker and the assistant chief with a Ford sedan; each carries a filter-type mask and is equipped with radio tuned to the police broadcast band.
Gadsden, AL	1937	The chief is provided with a Plymouth coupe.
Gainesville, FL	1955	The chief is provided with a 1950 Oldsmobile sedan, equipped with radio on the police system.
Galesburg, IL	1920	The chief is provided with a one-horse, rubber-tired buggy.
Galesburg, IL	1954	The chief is provided with a 1953 sedan.
Garfield, NJ	1945	The chief is provided with a Pontiac coupe equipped with 2-way radio and carrying first-aid and 2 hand extinguishers.
Gary, IN	1921	The chief is provided with a Cole roadster on which are carried 2 electric hand lights. At the time of the inspection this car was being painted and the reserve hose wagon was used instead.
Gary, IN	1927	The chief is provided with a Studebaker coupe, fitted with siren and electric hand lights; purchased in 1927. The mechanic uses his personal car.
Gary, IN	1932	The chief has a LaSalle coach and the assistant chief a Studebaker coupe which carries 3 inhalators, 2 smoke masks and a first-aid kit. The mechanic uses his own car.
Gastonia, NC	1955	Chief officers are provided with a radio equipped 1950 Chevrolet 4 door sedan, which is kept at headquarters at all times.
Glendale, CA	1937	The chief drives his own car to fires. The city provides a sedan of 1932 model for use of battalion chiefs, 3 touring cars for fire prevention work, hill patrol and shop use.
Gloucester, MA	1916	The chief is provided with a 4-passenger Knox automobile, carrying two three-gallon and tetrachloride extinguishers, ax, crow bar and electric search light.
Gloucester, MA	1956	The chief is provided with a 1952 Pontiac sedan which he takes home at night, leaving the deputy chief on duty without proper transportation.
Gloversville, NY	1926	A Chrysler 5 passenger automobile purchased in 1925 is provided for the chief.
Grand Forks, ND	1952	The chief is not provided with a car. He rides on pumper #1 while at the headquarters and uses his own car at other times. A 1939 Dodge quarter ton pick up truck is kept at headquarters for general use.
Granite City, IL	1931	The chief is provided with a Studebaker, 6-cylinder roadster, which carries a deluge set, an inhalator, a surgical kit, 2 gas masks, 2 gate valves, and a wye.
Granite City, IL	1938	The chief is provided with a 1938 Hudson sedan.
Great Falls, MT	1910	The chief is provided with a horse and wagon, used for general purposes as well as for responding to fires.
Great Falls, MT	1921	The chief is provided with a 4-passenger Stutz automobile which carries light equipment including two 3-gallon chemical extinguishers, gas masks, rope, electric hand lantern , ax and a lung motor.
Great Falls, MT	1950	A 1941 Buick coupe with 2-way radio on the police channel serves as the chief's car and auxiliary squad wagon. It carries soda-acid, foam CO2, pump-tank and back-pack extinguishers, gas masks, oxygen

breathing apparatus, brooms, shovels, bolt cutters, rope, life belts, stretcher, first-aid kit and when needed for first-aid calls, a resuscitator.

Great Falls, MT	1955	A 1953 DeSoto is used by the headquarters captain in responding to all fires. This car is radio-equipped and carries 6 gas masks, first-aid and rescue appliances and some additional items of minor equipment. The chief is provided with a 1951 Ford sedan, a 1941 Buick coupe is used by the fire inspector.
Green Bay, WI	1915	The chief is provided with a 30-horsepower White runabout, equipped with a 25-gallon chemical tank and 150 feet of chemical hose; a rubber-tired buggy and a cutter for winter use are in reserve.
Green Bay, WI	1929	A Buick roadster, purchased in 1924 is utilized by the chief officers.
Green Bay, WI	1955	A 1952 Pontiac sedan is provided for the chief officers use and is equipped with 3-way radio and carries a small extinguisher and one self-contained breathing apparatus.
Greensboro, NC	1925	The chief has a 2 passenger automobile which is his personal property. A small automobile is provided for general supply and fire alarm use.
Greensboro, NC	1936	The chief is provided with a Buick coupe.
Greensboro, NC	1951	A 1951 Pontiac and a 1946 Chevrolet 4 door sedans are provided for the chief and the assistant chief respectively. The assistant chief car carries a resuscitator, 2 self-contained breathing apparatus, an oxy-acetylene cutting torch, a 1-1/2 inch siphon. Both are equipped with two-way radios.
Greensboro, NC	1956	Two sedans for chief officers have been purchased and placed in service. The deputy chief on duty is provided with a 1952 Pontiac and the chief a 1955 Nash.
Greenville, SC	1959	A 1955 sedan, a 1958 station wagon and a 1954 sedan are provided for the chief, his assistants and the fire prevention inspectors.
Greenwich, CT	1928	A Studebaker and a Locomobile patrol are located in the Sound Beach and Borough stations, respectively, and are equipped with a squad body, and carry stretchers, rope, hose bridges and tarpaulins.
Greenwich, CT	1952	The chief is provided with a 1951 4-door DeSoto sedan, which is equipped with 2-way radio tuned to the police radio system.
Hackensack, NJ	1949	A 1949 Mercury sedan is provided for the chief, and a 1949 Mercury coupe is provided for the deputy chief on duty. Each car carries a gas mask and some minor appliances, and is equipped with 3-way radio.
Hamden, CT	1950	A Pontiac 2-door sedan equipped with two-way radio, is provided for the chief. The master mechanic has a 1-1/2-ton International truck which he uses as a supply truck and for fire alarm repairs. Both the chief's car and this truck have to be left outside the station daytimes as there is no room for them inside; they are taken home nights.
Hamilton, OH	1912	Both the chief and assistant chief have rubber-tired buggies, equipped with two portable extinguishers, a smoke protector, wire cutters and other small tools.
Hamilton, OH	1924	The chief and assistant chief are each provided with a Ford runabout, equipped with small delivery body.
Hamilton, OH	1930	The chief is provided with a Dodge roadster, purchased in 1924, and the assistant chief with a new Ford roadster.
Hammond, IN	1953	A Ford sedan is provided for the use of the chief, and another is available for fire department use; both are equipped with two-way radio. A sedan is provided for the fire prevention inspectors and a pickup truck for fire alarm use.
Hannibal, MO	1926	The chief is provided with a 5-passenger Jewett touring car.
Hannibal, MO	1947	A 1937 coach is provided for use of the chief. Assistant chiefs respond on apparatus.
Hartford, CT	1916	Chief's automobiles, 5 in service.
Hattiesburg, MS	1958	The chief is provided with a 1952 Chevrolet sedan, which is to be replaced in the near future.
Haverhill, MA	1914	The chief is provided with a 5-passenger Knox automobile with air-cooled motor; it is in only fair condition. A rubber-tired buggy, in poor condition, is held in reserve.
Haverhill, MA	1923	The chief is provided with a new Packard 5-passenger automobile in excellent condition.
Haverhill, MA	1927	The chief is provided with a Packard 5-passenger automobile. A Chandler touring car is used as general utility car by the department. A Ford truck is provided for repair and inspection work on the fire alarm system. A motor cycle, equipped with side car carrying 100 feet of 1/2-inch rubber hose, 2 three-gallon extinguishers, 4 one-quart carbon-tetrachloride extinguishers, ax and 2 brooms is stationed at headquarters. It responds to grass and automobile fires during the summer months, manned by two men from the headquarters company.
Haverhill, MA	1939	The chief is provided with a 1930 Packard sedan and the deputy chiefs with a 1934 Plymouth sedan.
Helena, MT	1910	The chief is provided with a horse and buggy.
Henderson, KY	1912	The chief is provided with a rubber tired runabout.
High Point, NC	1930	A 4-passenger Hudson roadster is provided for the chief.
High Point, NC	1954	Pontiac 4-door sedans, purchased in 1953 and 1948 respectively, are provided for the chief and assistant chief respectively.
Highland Park, MI	1927	The chief is provided with a Lincoln roadster equipped with 2 smoke masks, wrecking tool, lung motor and surgical kit.
Highland Park, MI	1959	The chief supplies his own transportation and the assistant chiefs use a 1958 station wagon.
Hoboken, NJ	1955	The chief is provided with a 1942 Cadillac 4-door sedan and the deputy chief with a 1954 Plymouth station wagon; both vehicles are three-way radio equipped and each carries a portable radio. An inhalator, a resuscitator, and a small amount of minor equipment are carried in the deputy chief's car.
Holyoke, MA	1915	The chief is provided with a 4-passenger, 36-horsepower Stevens-Duryea automobile. A 5-passenger, 54-horsepower Pope-Hartford automobile is provided for the deputy chiefs and the training of chauffeurs. A rubber-tired buggy with swinging harness, in fair condition, is in reserve.
Honolulu, HI	1941	Sedans are provided for the chief and first assistant chief and a coupe for the second assistant chief. 3 cars in service , 3 cars in reserve.

Honolulu, HI	1953	Five sedans, of Buick and Chrysler make and of 1948 model or later, are provided for the 5 chief officers, and a 1947 Buick is in reserve. Two Willys jeeps are available mainly for the drillmaster and for messengers.
Hot Springs, AR	1913	The chief is provided with a one-horse buggy.
Hot Springs, AR	1951	The chief is provided with a 1950 Chevrolet sedan.
Huntington Park, CA	1932	A Buick roadster of 1928 model is provided for the chief. Apparatus tanks are filled from a 50-gallon portable buggy at headquarters.
Huntington Park, CA	1952	A 1949 Ford sedan is provided for the chief, a 1949 Chevrolet for the assistant chief and a 1942 Plymouth for the battalion chief on duty, all equipped with 3-way radios.
Huntington, WV	1936	A Ford roadster is provided for the assistant chiefs.
Huntington, WV	1953	A 1948 DeSoto 4-door sedan and a 1950 Ford 2-door sedan are provided for the chief and assistant chief. A 1945 Chris-Craft cabin cruiser, 18 feet in length and powered with a Chrysler Marine engine, is docked on the Ohio River at the foot of 10th St.; no equipment of any kind is carried.
Huntsville, AL	1956	The chief is provided with a 1955 Chevrolet, 4-door sedan which he takes home at night. The assistant chief responds with one of the pumpers at headquarters. All apparatus including the chief's car is two-way radio equipped operating on the police department frequency.
Hutchinson, KS	1919	The chief is provided with a Ford runabout remodeled to carry four men, if necessary. It has no fire equipment, since the chief usually responds to fire alarms on the hose wagon.
Hutchinson, KS	1954	1949 Chrysler and 1949 Plymouth sedans are provided for the use of chief officers; each is equipped with a three-way police radio, and, in addition, carries a portable transmitter-receiver.
Ithaca, NY	1956	The chief and assistant chief on duty are provided with a 1956 Ford station wagon and a 1955 Ford station wagon; both vehicles are two-way radio equipped. No equipment is carried in the chief's car but a fair amount of minor equipment including two self contained breathing apparatus and an inhalator are carried in the assistant chief's car.
Jackson, MS	1914	The chief is provided with an automobile carrying 2 hand force-pumps, each in a 5-gallon portable tank, and a portable searchlight.
Jackson, MS	1924	The chief is provided with a Cadillac touring car.
Jackson, MS	1956	The chief is provided with a 1952 Buick 4-door sedan.
Jacksonville, FL	1907	Chief's wagons, 1 in service, 1 in reserve.
Jacksonville, FL	1951	There are 6 chief officers' cars in service. The chief is provided with a 1948 Cadillac 4-door sedan, the deputy chief a 1947 Ford sedan, two of the assistant chiefs have 1949 Mercury sedans, and two have 1946 Ford sedans. In addition, the fire marshal has a 1942 Chevrolet sedan and the chief fire inspector a 1942 Ford sedan. All of these cars are 3-way radio equipped except the chief inspectors. The assistant chiefs' cars have first-aid and spray kits, 2 filter type gas masks and a dry powder extinguisher.
Janesville, WI	1920	The chief has a 2-passenger Buick automobile purchased in 1910; it carries a 25-gallon chemical tank and 150 feet of chemical hose.
Janesville, WI	1959	The chief is provided with a 1956 sedan which carries a few items of minor equipment.
Jefferson City, MO	1948	A 1936 coupe is provided for the chief.
Jefferson Parish, LA	1956	The chief is provided with a radio-equipped 1953 Pontiac 2-door sedan.
Jersey City, NJ	1919	The commissioner and chief are each provided with a 7-passenger automobile. The deputy and each battalion chief has a two or four passenger automobile. The chief's and deputy chief's cars each carry a lung motor and each battalion chief's car a smoke protector. Dreger gas mask, portable electric light, wire cutters and rubber gloves.
Jersey City, NJ	1952	During this survey 10 Chevrolet sedans were purchased and delivered; one is provided for the commissioner, chief and each deputy and battalion chief on duty in the fire force; the remainder are assigned to non-fire force divisions in headquarters. Seven of the cars are equipped with the fire department 3-way FM radio.
Johnson City, TN	1937	The chief is provided with a 1937 Chevrolet closed car.
Johnson City, TN	1952	The chief is provided with a 1948 Chevrolet sedan. It is equipped with a inhalator, a gas mask, self-contained breathing apparatus, a salvage cover and two chemical extinguishers. The assistant chief responds to alarms in a privately-owned 1931 Ford sedan equipped with a chemical extinguisher.
Johnstown, PA	1914	The chief is provided with an automobile and has a rubber-tired buggy in reserve.
Johnstown, PA	1959	The chief is provided with a 1958 Chevrolet 4-door sedan. The assistant chiefs share the use of a 1956 Ford station wagon which carries a good variety of emergency and minor equipment.
Joliet, IL	1912	The fire marshal is provided with a rubber tired buggy.
Joliet, IL	1923	The chief is provided with a new Willys-Knight roadster.
Joliet, IL	1931	The chief is provided with an 8-cylinder Hupmobile roadster in good condition.
Joliet, IL	1956	The chief is provided with a 1953 four-door Packard sedan, which is not radio equipped.
Joplin, MO	1918	The chief is provided with a Chandler roadster, purchased in June, 1917. A 4-cylinder Oldsmobile, built in 1908, is in reserve for use as a supply and spare hose wagon.
Kalamazoo, MI	1912	The chief is provided with a buggy fitted with rubber tires; one is in reserve
Kalamazoo, MI	1939	The chief is provided with a 1938 sedan, and the assistant chief uses a 1934 coupe; each car is equipped with a two-way radio.
Kankakee, IL	1945	The chief is provided with a 1934 Ford coach which carries a 15-pound dry powder extinguisher, a small carbon-tetrachloride extinguisher and a gas mask.
Kansas City, KS	1913	The chief and one assistant are provided with automobiles; the second assistant chief is provided with a 1 horse buggy.

Kansas City, KS	1931	Three roadsters are provided for the chief and assistant chiefs on duty. A former chief's car rebuilt with a small truck body carries one fixed and one portable turret pipe with suitable tips.
Kenosha, WI	1920	Headquarters is where the chief's car, a 2-passenger Jeffery automobile, purchased in 1916 is kept. It carries two 3-gallon extinguishers.
Kenosha, WI	1958	A 1955 Nash sedan is provided for the use of the chief, and a 1953 Nash sedan is provided for the assistant chiefs. Each is equipped with a small fire extinguisher and filter-type gas mask.
Knoxville, TN	1929	A Buick sedan automobile is provided for the chief and a Studebaker runabout for the assistant chief on duty.
Knoxville, TN	1941	The chief is provided with a 1940 Chevrolet sedan and the assistant chiefs with a 1936 Plymouth coupe, both with police radio receivers.
Knoxville, TN	1947	The chief is provided with a 1946 Ford sedan and the assistant chiefs with a 1940 Chevrolet coach, both equipped with police radio receivers.
Kokomo, IN	1940	The chief is provided with a 1939 Ford coupe and an old 1929 Chrysler coupe is available for alarms and emergency calls, and is equipped with two-way radio.
Kokomo, IN	1951	Sedans are provided for the use of the chief and the fire prevention inspector. A 1947 Ford ambulance at headquarters is used by the assistant chiefs in responding to alarms. A pickup truck is provided for fire alarm and general use. The chief's car and the ambulance are equipped with three-way radio.
La Crosse, WI	1911	The chief and the electrician are provided with buggies.
La Crosse, WI	1932	The chief is provided with an old Pierce-Arrow touring car that carries an ax, 2 chemical extinguishers, hand pump, wire cutters, rubber gloves, first-aid kit, 3 gas masks, inhalator and salvage cover. Two Pierce-Arrow touring cars are in reserve; a motorcycle with side car is available for department use.
Lackawanna, NY	1953	The chief is provided with a 1949 Studebaker 2-door sedan. Fuel is carried to fires in ordinary cans, usually in the chief's car by available personnel.
Lafayette, IN	1922	The chief officer on duty uses a 2-passenger automobile, purchased in 1915, equipped with two 2-1/2-gallon chemical extinguishers, a burst-hose jacket, shut-off nozzle and a gas mask. It is in poor condition. A small 2-passenger automobile is used for the delivery of supplies and for fire alarm work.
Lafayette, LA	1958	An International 1/2-ton pickup truck, in service at headquarters, is used for transportation by the assistant chiefs. The chief used his personal automobile for transportation.
Lake Charles, LA	1952	A 1951 Dodge sedan is provided for the chief and a 1947 Chevrolet sedan for the assistant chiefs; each is equipped with a filter-type gas mask.
Lakeland, FL	1955	The chief is provided with a 1953 Buick 4-door sedan; it is radio equipped and carries one carbon dioxide extinguisher and one filter-type gas mask.
Lakewood, OH	1922	The chief is provided with a Pierce-Arrow touring car, purchased in 1919, carrying 1 Pyrene extinguisher. One 2-ton Cadillac supply automobile is provided.
Lakewood, OH	1928	The chief is provided with a Pierce-Arrow touring car, purchased in 1927 and the assistant chief with a Ford roadster, purchased in 1926.
Lancaster, OH	1950	A 1947 Chevrolet enclosed-body utility truck, equipped with two-way radio tuned to the police frequency, is in service at headquarters. The chief responds to alarms with this apparatus during the day and by private automobile at night.
Lancaster, PA	1909	The chief has a two-wheel cart at Engine No. 5 and a buggy at his residence. The former is only used to respond to fires in outlying districts or to sections not covered by No. 5, one of the horses assigned to Engine No. 5 being used.
Lancaster, PA	1917	The chief is provided with a 2-passenger Overland automobile, which carries a 1-quart and two 3-gallon extinguishers and a searchlight.
Lancaster, PA	1955	A 1952 and two 1947 Dodge business coupes are provided for the chief and two assistant chiefs, respectively; all are 3-way radio equipped.
Lansing, MI	1911	The chief has an automobile. A horse-drawn buggy is in reserve.
Las Vegas, NV	1958	A 1953 DeSoto sedan is provided for the chief, a 1957 Chevrolet sedan for the assistant chief, a 1950 Chevrolet coupe for the battalion chiefs, a 1953 Chevrolet sedan for the fire marshal, and a 1959 Chevrolet and a 1955 Ford for the fire prevention inspectors. A 1954 Chevrolet panel truck is used for resuscitator calls and, at fires, as a communications center or ambulance for injured firemen. City regulations forbid its use as an ambulance for the general public.
Lawrence, MA	1908	Four hose sleighs, three chief's sleighs and hub runners for other apparatus are provided but are seldom needed.
Lawrence, MA	1922	Two 5-passenger Paige automobiles are provided for the use of the chief and deputy chief.
Lawton, OK	1948	A 1947 Ford sedan is provided for use by the chief, the assistant chief responds on apparatus.
Lebanon, PA	1953	A 1952 Plymouth, 2-door coupe, owned by the city is provided for the chief.
Levittown, NY	1952	A Ford sedan is provided for the chief. The car is provided with a 3 way radio tuned to the fire department wave length.
Lewiston, ME	1907	Chief's wagon, 1 in service.
Lewiston, ME	1926	The chief is provided with a Studebaker roadster; it carries a deluge set and gas mask.
Lewiston, ME	1952	The chief is provided with a 1951 Pontiac 4-door sedan. When the chief is at home the car is left at headquarters for the deputy chief on duty to use.
Lexington, KY	1910	Chief's wagon, 1 in service.
Lima, OH	1912	The chief has a rubber-tired buggy.
Lima, OH	1921	There is a Willys-Knight roadster for the use of the chief. The assistant chief rides with the hose wagon.
Lima, OH	1925	The chief is provided with a Cadillac touring car carrying 50 ft. of 1-inch hose, two 3-gallon chemical extinguishers, 2 Burrell smoke masks, 1 lung motor, 1 wire cutters, 4 waterproof covers and a hydrant pump.

Lima, OH	1953	A 1951 Oldsmobile sedan is provided for use of the chief and assistant chiefs; it is equipped with two-way radio, tuned to police radio frequency.
Lincoln, NE	1922	The chief is provided with a 5-passenger touring car of late model, which carries 2 chemical extinguishers, a small first-aid kit and a gas mask. The assistant chief is provided with a light roadster, carrying a chemical extinguisher and a plaster hook.
Lincoln, NE	1957	The chief and assistant and battalion chiefs are provided with Oldsmobile 4-door sedans.
Little Rock, AR	1911	The chief is provided with an automobile, which carries two 3-gallon chemical extinguishers. There is a chief's buggy in reserve, which is sometimes used by the first assistant chief.
Little Rock, AR	1923	The chief is furnished with a Dodge runabout; the first assistant chief responds to fires in a Ford, owned by himself but maintained by the city. A Cadillac automobile with platform body is used by the master mechanic and fire alarm electrician as a supply and repair wagon; it is equipped with 2 hand chemical tanks, ax and nozzle; when needed it is loaded with about 600 feet of hose and used as a spare hose wagon.
Little Rock, AR	1931	The chief is provided with a Dodge 8-cylinder sedan and the assistant chiefs each have a Dodge 6-cylinder coupe. There are no other cars.
Lockport, NY	1911	The chief furnishes his horse and the city furnishes his buggy and harness,
Lockport, NY	1953	A 1947 Oldsmobile sedan equipped with 3 way radio is used by the chief; it carries an inhalator, two electric hand lights, and a few minor appliances.
Logansport, IN	1928	The chief is provided with a Dodge roadster.
Long Beach, CA	1922	The chief is provided with a 4-passenger Studebaker automobile and the assistant chief with a Buick 2-passenger roadster; the latter carries two 2-1/2-gallon chemical extinguishers and a lungmotor.
Long Beach, CA	1926	A Cadillac touring car is provided for the chief, a Peerless roadster for the assistant chief and two Jordan roadsters for the district chiefs, with a second Peerless roadster in reserve. Two light touring cars are furnished to the Fire Prevention Bureau.
Lorain, OH	1942	The chief is provided with a coach. A reconverted 1931 Ford carries water cans, extinguishers, and some minor equipment and is used for response to known minor fires and for department errands.
Los Angeles, CA	1910	1 automobile in service, Buggies, 5 in service, 1 in reserve.
Los Angeles, CA	1917	Chief's and other autos, 7 in service, 2 in reserve; Chief's and Hydrant Buggies, 3 in service, 2 in reserve.
Los Angeles, CA	1924	Touring cars are provided for Chief Scott, Assistant Chiefs Davis and McDowell and the Fire Prevention Bureau. In each district is a roadster for the use of battalion chiefs, and a second used for hydrant inspections; 3 battalion chief's roadsters are in reserve. The store room force has 7 roadsters, 3 light delivery wagons and two 2-ton trucks. Chiefs cars carry first-aid equipment. Chief's and other autos, 25 in service, 3 in reserve.
Los Angeles, CA	1928	Touring cars are furnished for chief, deputy and first assistants, roadsters for district chiefs, master mechanic, mountain patrols, fire prevention inspectors, arson investigators and hydrant inspectors. 66 in service and 6 in reserve.
Los Angeles, CA	1947	Buick sedans of 1947 model are furnished to chief officers on duty and heads of bureaus. 53 in service, 4 in reserve.
Louisville, KY	1915	The city provides a 5-passenger Packard car for the chief, a 2-passenger automobile for the master mechanic, a 4-passenger Cadillac automobile for the chief operator and a light buggy for each assistant chief.
Louisville, KY	1933	The chief is provided with a 7-passenger Packard touring car; other chief officers are each provided with a 6-cylinder roadster; one roadster is in reserve.
Lowell, MA	1908	Sleighs are provided for the use of the chief, fire alarm operator, protective company and six of the hose and engine companies. Chief's wagons, 3 in service.
Lynchburg, VA	1921	The chief is provided with a five-passenger automobile, kept at headquarters. This car carries four 3-gallon portable extinguishers, a portable electric searchlight and a smoke mask; it is in poor condition and not worth repairing.
Lynchburg, VA	1930	The chief is provided with a 5-passenger, 6-cylinder Dodge automobile carrying 2-extinguishers, ax, crowbar, rubber gloves and gas mask.
Lynchburg, VA	1955	A 1950 Oldsmobile four-door sedan is provided for use by the assistant chief; it is equipped with a small amount of emergency and minor equipment. A 1954 Chevrolet four-door sedan is provided for use by the chief.
Macon, GA	1955	A 1953 DeSoto sedan is provided for the chief, two 1950 Ford sedans for the district chiefs on duty and a 1953 Plymouth sedan for the Bureau of Fire Prevention. All automobiles are equipped with three-way radio and the three chiefs' cars also carry a small, portable transmitter-receiver.
Manchester, CT	1951	The chief is provided with a 1948 Buick 4-door sedan which carries a dry powder extinguisher, a filter type gas mask, handlight and a small amount of other minor equipment. A 1946 Hudson 1/2-ton pickup truck is provided for the joint use of the master mechanic and the superintendent of fire alarm and if available, would be sent with 1 or 2 men to all fires.
Manitowoc, WI	1931	The chief is provided with a 1926 model, 6-cylinder Nash roadster.
Manitowoc, WI	1938	The chief is provided with a 1927 Cadillac, 3-passenger coupe. No other automobile equipment is provided.
Mansfield, OH	1926	The chief is provided with a touring car equipped with a chemical extinguisher, a short ladder, surgical kit, pulmotor, 2 Burrell smoke masks, cellar pipe, wire cutters, shovel, rubber gloves, gas key, rope and 2 waterproof covers. The car is used for non-building and chimney fires and is manned by men from headquarters company.

Mansfield, OH	1954	A 1954 Oldsmobile is provided for use of the chief and a 1950 Ford for the assistant chiefs. Both cars are equipped with two way radios tuned to the police radio frequency. A station wagon is provided for general use.
Marion, IN	1927	The chief is provided with a Studebaker roadster which carries an extra 40-gallon gasoline tank for the purpose of supplying apparatus tanks.
Marion, OH	1959	A 1955 Pontiac station wagon is provided for use by the chief.
Massillon, OH	1928	The chief has a 2-passenger Buick automobile.
Maywood, IL	1944	The fire chief drives a 1941 Graham sedan which is privately owned but which is maintained by the village.
McKeesport, PA	1925	The chief is provided with a 6-cylinder Buick roadster automobile, ordinarily stationed at headquarters.
McKeesport, PA	1933	The chief has a Chandler roadster.
Memphis, TN	1925	The chief is provided with a Cadillac 1925 touring car; each assistant chief , master mechanic and fire marshal are supplied with Ford roadsters. Chief's automobiles, 5 in service.
Meridian, MS	1914	The chief has an iron-tired buggy in reserve; no horse is provided for this. The chief and assistant chief go to fires on the automobile of Hose 1.
Meridian, MS	1924	The chief and assistant chief ride to fires in a Dodge roadster. This car and a Ford truck would also be used in case of emergency for delivery of gasoline to apparatus at fires.
Meridian, MS	1953	The chief is provided with a 1948 Pontiac 4-door sedan which is radio equipped but carries no minor equipment. This car is left at headquarters at night for use by the assistant chief on duty.
Miami Beach, FL	1951	A 1946 Buick sedan is provided for the chief and a 1946 Chrysler for the battalion captain on duty; both are equipped with two-way radio.
Miami, FL	1921	The chief and the assistant chief are each provided with a 4- or 5-passenger automobile. The assistant chief's car is equipped with a 35-gallon chemical tank, 150 feet of chemical hose, ax and 2 hand extinguishers.
Miami, FL	1960	The chief and the assistant chief are provided with 1956 and 1957 4-door sedans, respectively. District chiefs are provided with a 1957 and two 1956 station wagons, and eleven 1949 to 1958 sedans or coupes and a 1953 station wagon are assigned to various activities including the fire prevention bureau, fire college, maintenance shops, fire alarm operations section, and high pressure system.
Middletown, CT	1954	A 1949 Buick 4-door sedan, equipped with a three-way radio, is provided for the chief of the Middletown department.
Middletown, OH	1952	The chief is provided with a 1950 Chevrolet sedan and a 1946 Chevrolet sedan is furnished for the use of the assistant chiefs.
Milwaukee, WI	1912	Chief's automobiles, 7 in service, 1 in reserve, Chief's wagons, 8 in reserve.
Milwaukee, WI	1929	The chief, each assistant chief, the superintendent of machinery and apparatus, the foreman of the repair shop, drill master and fire prevention bureau are provided with automobiles; 4 automobiles are in reserve.
Milwaukee, WI	1956	The chief, the assistant chief and the deputy chiefs are furnished with 1954-55 Oldsmobile 4-door sedans, and all battalion chiefs with 1949-53 Pontiac 4-door sedans. Three cars and a station wagon are assigned to the Bureau of Fire Prevention and Protection, 3 cars to the Bureau of Instruction and Training, and 2 cars to the maintenance force; 4 cars are in reserve. A fully-equipped ambulance was donated to the Dept. in 1947 by a Firebuffs Club and is in good condition.
Mishawaka, IN	1929	The chief is provided with an Auburn touring car purchased in 1926; equipment includes 2 foam extinguishers.
Mobile, AL	1904	Chief's wagons, 2 in service.
Mobile, AL	1950	Seven automobiles are provided; 4 are used by chief officers on duty, 2 by off-duty chief officers for responding on call and one by the fire prevention inspector. The cars used by the four chief officers on duty are equipped with 2-way FM radio on the police frequency; three carry self-contained breathing apparatus. A 1935 Oldsmobile has been cut down for use as a truck.
Moline, IL	1921	The chief is provided with a 2-passenger, Velie car, purchased in 1920.
Moline, IL	1930	The chief is provided with a 2-passenger Velie coupe purchased in 1928. No equipment is carried. An old Velie, formerly used by the chief, has been converted into a supply truck and is also used on fire alarm work. The chief's car is in good condition; the supply truck is in poor condition.
Montgomery, AL	1907	Chief's wagon, 1 in service. Fully paid since 1898.
Montgomery, AL	1914	The chief is provided with an automobile and has a rubber-tired buggy in reserve; the assistant chief has a rubber-tired buggy.
Mount Vernon, NY	1957	A 1952 DeSoto 4-door sedan is provided for the chief; a 1955 Dodge 4-door sedan for the deputy chief on duty. A 1952 Plymouth coupe for the volunteer deputy chief on call and two 1952 Plymouth coupes for fire prevention work. A small amount of minor equipment is carried in the cars. All cars are equipped with 3 way radios. In addition a small portable radio is carried in the chief cars for communications on the fire ground.
Muncie, IN	1956	1954 Mercury and 1947 Oldsmobile 4-door sedans are provided for the chief and the assistant chiefs, respectively; the latter carries one self-contained mask, and both are equipped with two-way radio.
Muskegon, MI	1955	The chief is provided with a 1953 Chevrolet sedan and a 1951 Ford sedan is provided for the use of the assistant and battalion chiefs.
N. Bergen, NJ	1956	The chief is provided with a 1952 Mercury 4-door sedan while a 1951 Chevrolet 4-door sedan, equipped with a small amount of minor equipment and an inhalator, is provided for the deputy chief on duty; both vehicles are 3-way radio equipped. A 1946 Chevrolet 2-door business coupe and a 1948 Chevrolet 4-door sedan are provided for use by the fire prevention inspectors.
N. Little Rock, AR	1938	The chief is provided with a 1936 Ford coupe.

N. Little Rock, AR	1947	A 1941 Ford coupe, painted black and without a police radio is provided for the chief.
Nashua, NH	1950	A 1946 Dodge sedan is provided for the chief and a 1948 Plymouth sedan for the deputy chief. Both cars are 2-way radio equipped.
Nashville, TN	1956	Nine late model sedans are provided for use of the chief, assistant and battalion chiefs, drillmaster, fire marshal, assistant fire marshal, superintendent of shop, and superintendent of fire alarm; one sedan is in reserve.
New Albany, IN	1920	The chief's one-horse, rubber-tired buggy carries a crow-bar, smoke mask, nozzle tip, hand electric searchlight and lantern. A one-horse, iron-tired wagon serves as a supply wagon and replaces hose wagons that are out of service.
New Albany, IN	1928	The chief is provided with a Nash roadster.
New Albany, IN	1946	The chief is provided with a 1942 Studebaker coach.
New Bedford, MA	1953	There are six chief officer's cars in service and one in reserve. The chief is provided with a 1949 Ford 4-door sedan while the following vehicles are assigned to the district chiefs; a 1949 Ford 4-door sedan, a 1948 Ford 2-door sedan, two 1942 Chevrolet 2-door coupes and a 1941 Ford 2-door coupe. All vehicles are 3-way radio equipped. A 1950 Ford 4-door sedan is in reserve at the repair shop.
New Britain, CT	1958	A 1957 Buick, 4-door sedan is provided for the chief, a 1958 Ford station wagon is provided for the assistant and deputy chiefs and a 1953 Ford, 4-door sedan is provided for the fire prevention bureau.
New Brunswick, NJ	1957	The chief is provided with a 1956 Chrysler 4-door sedan; a small amount of minor equipment is carried. The Fire Prevention Bureau is provided with a 1950 Chrysler 4-door sedan.
New Castle, PA	1914	The chief is provided with a Ford runabout carrying 2 portable extinguishers, ax, crowbar, brace and bits, saw, hatchet, and hand torch.
New Castle, PA	1953	Chief officers are provided with a 1948 Dodge radio-equipped, business coupe.
New London, CT	1923	The chief is provided with a Chevrolet roadster. With Engine 1 and Hose 6 are automobile squad wagons which are used to pick up volunteer members on the way to fires.
New London, CT	1951	The chief is provided with a 1938 Cadillac coupe which is equipped with a 2-way FM radio and a fair amount of minor equipment. A 1942 Ford 2-door sedan is provided for the fire marshal. This is also 2-way FM radio equipped but carries no minor equipment.
New Orleans, LA	1915	The chief and two assistant engineers are provided with automobiles; seven 1 horse buggies are provided for assistant engineers use, and one is in reserve.
New Orleans, LA	1956	The superintendent, the assistant superintendent, and the district chiefs are provided with late model sedans. 10 cars in service.
New Rochelle, NY	1915	The city provides an automobile for the chief. The assistant chiefs have their private cars; a light wagonette at engine #1 could be used as a chief's buggy. The chief's car carries a water tight light, search lights, surgical kits and 2-1/2 gallon extinguisher.
New Rochelle, NY	1957	Two 1952 Oldsmobile 4-door sedans equipped with two way radios are provided for the chief and battalion chiefs respectively. Each carries a small amount of minor equipment including breathing apparatus.
New York City, NY	1929	Automobiles are provided for the commissioner, deputy commissioner, all chief officers on duty, heads of the bureau of repair and supplies, fire prevention, fire investigation, and fire alarm telegraph. Two Mack wrecking trucks are kept at the repair shop.
Newark, NJ	1952	The chief and each deputy and battalion chief on duty are provided with a 4-door sedan. In addition, twelve other sedans are provided for the use of various other divisions within the department. All of the cars used by chief officers have 2-way radios tuned to the police radio system. Each of the chief's cars in the fire force is equipped with a carbon dioxide extinguisher, one filter-type gas mask, one self-contained breathing apparatus, one inhalator-resuscitator, a first-aid kit and a spray nozzle for 2-1/2- inch hose. There are five chief's cars in reserve.
Newark, OH	1912	The chief keeps own car at the headquarters.
Newark, OH	1956	A 1953 radio-equipped tudor sedan is provided for the use of the chief and carries a carbon dioxide extinguisher.
Newburgh, NY	1928	Four part-paid volunteer chiefs; the master mechanic sleeps at station #4 and responds to all alarms usually acting as the chief's driver.
Newport News, VA	1922	The chief is provided with a Buick roadster carrying a distributing nozzle and 2 gas masks.
Newport News, VA	1957	The chief and assistant chief on duty are provided with a 1950 Oldsmobile 4-door sedan and a 1950 Chevrolet 4-door sedan, respectively. At the time of the survey the department was awaiting delivery of a 1957 Oldsmobile sedan for use as a chief's car. A small amount of miscellaneous minor equipment is carried in both cars; each is 3-way radio equipped.
Newport, KY	1922	The chief is provided with a Cadillac roadster.
Newport, KY	1929	The chief is provided with a Ford Roadster purchased in 1929.
Newton, MA	1941	The chief and the assistant chief each has a Buick automobile equipped with 2-way radio. Each car carries some minor equipment which includes 2 gas masks, first-aid kit, telephone head set, sprinkler heads, hand fire extinguishers, rubber and asbestos gloves, and a water map.
Norristown, PA	1947	A sedan, equipped with a two-way radio, is provided for the chief. A coupe is provided for the assistant chief of the Norris Company; minor equipment carried in each car includes an all-service gas mask, asbestos suit, rope gun, and spray kit for burns.
North Tonawanda, NY	1915	Chief's conveyance- The city does not provide any conveyance for the chief. The present chief uses his own automobile.
North Tonawanda, NY	1952	A 1941 Chevrolet coupe is provided for the use of the chief and a 1950 Pontiac metal station wagon for the assistant chiefs. The station wagon is equipped with a resuscitator, two 15 minute self contained breathing

apparatus, a foam aspirating nozzle for attachment to a booster line with 5 gallons of liquid foam and some minor equipment.

Norwalk, CT	1928	The chief is provided with a Buick roadster which carries two 2-1/2-gallon foam-type extinguishers, hose shut-off, 3 pairs of rubber gloves, 2 gas masks, 2 portable electric lights and a first-aid kit.
Norwalk, CT	1953	The chief and deputy chief on duty are each provided with a 4-door sedan. The chief has a 1952 Packard and the deputy chief a 1939 Oldsmobile. Both cars are 3-way radio equipped. The chief's car is equipped with 2 filter-type gas masks, a soda and acid extinguisher, a first-aid kit, 5 sprinkler heads and some small tools. The deputy's car is equipped with a 500-watt fixed electric generator, a 250-watt floodlight, 150 feet of electric cable, a self-contained breathing apparatus, 2 filter type gas masks, a knapsack type pump tank, soda and acid extinguisher, 2 first-aid kits and other small tools.
Norwich, CT	1954	A 1950 Ford 4-door sedan and a 1951 Plymouth 2-door sedan are provided for the chief and deputy chief, respectively; both cars are radio equipped.
Norwood, OH	1955	A 1950 Oldsmobile club coupe is provided for the chief and a 1949 Chevrolet two-door sedan for the marshal's use; both carry an extinguisher and a hydrant wrench, and the latter has two filter-type masks.
Oak Park, IL	1923	The chief is provided with a 5-passenger Reo purchased in 1919; it carries no fire-fighting equipment.
Oak Park, IL	1926	The chief is provided with a 5-passenger Hudson touring car purchased in 1923. It carries no fire-fighting equipment.
Oak Park, IL	1947	The chief is provided with a 1947 Buick sedan, equipped with two-way radio. A 1937 Ford coupe is provided for the use of the fire prevention inspector.
Oak Park, MI	1959	The director, marshal, detectives and juvenile officers are provided with late model sedans. The marshal's car carries a self-contained breathing apparatus, an amplifying speaker, explosion meter and extinguishers, and the director's car carries a filter-type gas mask and extinguisher. All vehicles are equipped with sirens and warning lights.
Oakland, CA	1926	Touring cars are provided for the chief and assistant chiefs; 9 roadsters are furnished for district chiefs, the fire prevention bureau, superintendent of engines and hydrant inspector, one being in reserve. A Reo speed wagon is used for shop work.
Ogden, UT	1931	A 1924 Buick roadster model is provided for the chief; it carries chemical extinguishers and gas masks.
Ogden, UT	1940	The city provides for the chief an open Auburn speedster of recent model which because of limited storage space carries only a hydrant wrench and two gas masks. A Buick coupe of older model is used when answering inhalator calls.
Ogden, UT	1954	The chief has a 1951 Packard club coupe and the fire prevention bureau has two 4-door sedans, one a 1951 Chevrolet and the other a 1942 Dodge. The battalion chiefs use a 1952 Ford pickup for responding to alarms as well as for routine driving; it carries two 30-pound dry chemical extinguishers, and it is planned to install a booster pump and 150-gallon water tank.
Omaha, NE	1913	The chief is provided with an automobile, carrying a 3-gallon portable extinguisher. The first and second assistant chiefs are provided with rubber-tired buggies. One chief's buggy is in reserve.
Orange, NJ	1934	The chief is provided with a Buick roadster.
Orlando, FL	1927	The chief has his own roadster and sedan, and the assistant chief and 4 lieutenants each have Fords that are used for fire service.
Orlando, FL	1952	A 1950 Buick 4-door, radio-equipped, sedan is provided for the use of the chief and carries some minor equipment.
Oshkosh, WI	1926	The chief is provided with a 7-passenger Studebaker touring car, carrying two 2-1/2-gallon chemical extinguishers.
Oshkosh, WI	1932	The chief is provided with a 2-passenger Studebaker automobile, carrying two 2-1/2-gallon chemical extinguishers.
Oshkosh, WI	1937	The chief is provided with a 1926 Studebaker roadster.
Oswego, NY	1908	The department now owns eleven horses and hires two. The number does not provide for the chief's buggy nor give any reserve horses.
Oswego, NY	1938	The chief only is provided with a car. The fire department auxiliary has a sedan and 2 motorcycles.
Oswego, NY	1956	The chief is provided with a 1950 Buick 4-door sedan; no equipment is carried. No transportation is provided for the assistant chief on duty.
Ottumwa, IA	1926	The chief is provided with a 6-cylinder, 2-passenger Buick car, purchased in 1919, carrying a 30-gallon chemical tank and 200 feet of 3/4-inch chemical hose.
Ottumwa, IA	1932	The chief is provided with a 6-cylinder Hudson roadster carrying some minor equipment.
Ottumwa, IA	1952	The chief is provided with a 1950 Oldsmobile 4-door sedan, equipped with a 3-way radio.
Paducah, KY	1924	The chief is provided with a 4-passenger high-speed Stutz automobile, equipped with two 3-gallon chemical extinguishers, one Pyrene extinguisher and four 12x12 waterproof covers.
Paducah, KY	1930	The chief is provided with a Hudson coupe. A Ford roadster is utilized by the fire alarm superintendent.
Paducah, KY	1954	A 1950 Oldsmobile sedan is provided for the chief; it is equipped with a small carbon dioxide extinguisher and one salvage cover.
Parkersburg, WV	1920	The chief is provided with a 2-passenger automobile, carrying a 50-gallon chemical tank with a 2-1/2-inch hose connection and 250 feet of 1-inch hose, 6 chemical extinguishers, 1 ax, 1 door opener and a smoke protector.
Parkersburg, WV	1950	A 1948 Chevrolet 4-door sedan, radio-equipped, is provided for the chief.
Pasadena, CA	1934	The chief drives his personal car which is equipped with radio receiver tuned to the police transmitter.
Passaic, NJ	1950	The chief is provided with a 1940 Buick sedan and the deputy and battalion chief on duty are each provided with a 1942 Chevrolet sedan.

Paterson, NJ	1913	Each of the chiefs is provided with an automobile carrying a 3-gallon portable extinguisher; in addition, the chief's automobile carries a distributing nozzle, "Electrine" extinguisher and a smoke mask.
Paterson, NJ	1954	There are four chief officers' cars in service. The chief is provided with a 1952 Buick four-door sedan; when he is off duty, the car is kept at headquarters and in the event of an alarm to which the chief would respond, his driver would call for him. A 1951 and two 1950 Ford four-door sedans are provided for the 1st battalion chief, deputy chief and 2nd battalion chief; each vehicle carries one self-contained breathing apparatus.
Pawtucket, RI	1908	Chief's wagons, 1 in service.
Pawtucket, RI	1917	The chief is provided with a National automobile, which has a special body to carry an auxiliary squad. It carries 2 chemical extinguishers, 2 lanterns, nozzle, 2 axes, and 100 feet of rope.
Pawtucket, RI	1928	A Reo coupe is provided for the use of the chief.
Pawtucket, RI	1950	A 1946 Oldsmobile sedan is provided for the chief and a 1946 Chevrolet sedan for the two deputy chiefs. The chief's car carries no minor equipment other than a two-way radio. The deputy chief's car carries some minor equipment, including an inhalator and a fresh-air mask and a radio receiver.
Pensacola, FL	1950	Three Chevrolet sedans are provided for the use of the chief, the assistant chief on duty and the fire prevention inspector.
Peoria, IL	1915	The chief is provided with an Interstate automobile runabout and each of the assistant chiefs with a rubber-tired buggy, with one in reserve.
Peoria, IL	1923	The chief is provided with a 1918 Cadillac runabout, and the assistant chief has a 1920 Stearns-Knight runabout, both of which are in good condition. All apparatus is equipped with a green light mounted high on the machine as a warning to street traffic.
Peoria, IL	1928	The chief is provided with a 1925 Cadillac runabout, and the assistant chief has a 1925 Studebaker runabout, both of which are in good condition.
Peoria, IL	1937	The marshal is provided with a 1937 Chevrolet coupe equipped with a two-way radio. The assistant marshals have an older Chevrolet coupe and a Ford sedan.
Perth Amboy, NJ	1924	The city mechanic, provided with a touring car equipped with a flood and spot light and kit of tools, picks up the chief and responds to all alarms.
Perth Amboy, NJ	1956	The paid chief is provided with a 1955 Oldsmobile 4-door sedan and the volunteer chief is provided with a radio equipped, 1954 Plymouth 4-door sedan. A 1953 Dodge 4-door sedan is assigned for use by the fire prevention inspectors.
Petersburg, VA	1907	Chief's wagons, 1 in service.
Petersburg, VA	1950	A 1947 Pontiac sedan equipped with two-way radio is furnished to the chief and a 1940 Ford 1/2-ton pickup truck is provided for fire department general use.
Phoenix, AZ	1927	A Hudson touring car is provided for the chief; the inspector uses a Ford and the assistant chief, a motorcycle.
Phoenix, AZ	1938	A 1934 sedan, with two-way radio, is furnished for use of the deputy and assistant chiefs. A 1934 coupe with radio receiver for the chief, a 1928 model Ford roadster for the fire marshal and the fire alarm superintendent and a roadster and touring car are provided for general utility and reserve service.
Pine Bluff, AR	1938	The chief officers use their private cars for departmental use; they are black and like the fire apparatus, lack distinguishing lights for operating through traffic.
Pine Bluff, AR	1949	The chief is provided with a 1949 Chevrolet sedan, equipped with 2-way radio. A 1942 Chevrolet sedan is provided for the use of the assistant chief.
Pittsburgh, PA	1915	The city provides a 4-passenger Knox automobile for the chief, and a 2-passenger Overland automobile for each assistant chief; the auto mechanician has a horse and buggy. Several light buggies are in reserve. 10 cars in reserve.
Pittsburgh, PA	1923	9 cars in service.
Pittsburgh, PA	1952	A 1949 Cadillac sedan is used by the chief and seven 1950 Ford coupes are provided for the use of deputy and battalion chiefs. The chief of the river patrol has a 1947 Plymouth coupe, and a 1947 Ford 2-door sedan is used by the captain in charge of training. A 1949 Ford coupe is in reserve. All passenger cars are equipped with 2-way radio tuned to the police broadcast system, and chiefs' cars carry one or two self-contained breathing apparatus equipped with telephones, 2 approved filter-type gas masks, hand lights, first-aid kit and a small extinguisher.
Pittsfield, MA	1914	The chief is provided with an automobile and has a rubber-tired buggy in reserve.
Plainfield, NJ	1956	The chief is provided with a 1952 Chevrolet 4-door sedan and the deputy chief on duty with a 1952 Chevrolet coupe; both are 3-way radio equipped and carry a portable transmitter-receiver, and the deputy chief's car also has a public address loudspeaker. A filter-type mask, a self-contained breathing apparatus and a small amount of minor equipment are kept in each car.
Pocatello, ID	1955	A 1949 Pontiac panel truck with a 55-gallon water tank, a small pump and 150 feet of garden hose is used by the battalion chief in responding to fires. It also carries some emergency and minor equipment.
Pomona, CA	1949	A Pontiac coupe is provided for the chief. A sedan is loaded with first aid equipment. Two cars are provided for fire inspectors.
Pontiac, MI	1958	A 1957 Pontiac 2-door sedan is provided for the chief and a 1957 Pontiac station wagon, received during the survey, for the assistant chief. A 1950 Pontiac 2-door sedan is assigned to the fire marshal.
Port Huron, MI	1919	The chief has a two-passenger automobile.
Portsmouth, NH	1951	A 1942 Pontiac 2-door sedan is provided for the chief and is equipped with a 2-way radio.
Portsmouth, OH	1912	The chief is provided with a buggy having rubber tires.
Portsmouth, OH	1956	A 1952 Chevrolet sedan and a 1950 Chevrolet panel truck are provided for the chief and assistant chief, respectively.

Portsmouth, VA	1950	An automobile is provided for the chief, the assistant chief on duty and the fire prevention inspector. The 2 chief officers' cars are radio-equipped. Four men are assigned to the assistant chief's car to respond to all fires.
Pottsville, PA	1915	A Maxwell touring car is provided, in only fair condition. In addition to being used for fire service, it is also used as a patrol wagon by the police department and for hauling small supplies and tools for the highway department.
Pottsville, PA	1957	A 1951 Studebaker 2-door sedan, owned by the city, is provided for the chief. It is equipped with a 3-way radio on the police department system and carries a small amount of minor equipment.
Poughkeepsie, NY	1911	The chief is elected for a 2 year term by the firemen. The assistant chiefs are appointed by the chief and hold office during his pleasure. One chief's wagon recorded. Nine horses are owned by the companies; one engine is not provided with horses, dependence is placed on a team furnished by a contractor several blocks from the station.
Poughkeepsie, NY	1950	A 1941 Chevrolet sedan, two way radio equipped is provided for the chief.
Providence, RI	1912	The chief is provided with an automobile. Each district chief makes use of a rubber-tired buggy.
Providence, RI	1941	Five automobiles are provided for use of chief officers; four are each equipped with a radio receiving set. Equipment carried on battalion chiefs' cars includes an inhalator, gas mask, oxygen mask, sprinkler heads, telephone headset and first-aid kit; a motion picture camera and film are carried in the chief's car.
Pueblo, CO	1933	The 3 chief officers have coupes, ordinarily stationed at headquarters.
Quincy, IL	1910	The chief's buggy is privately owned.
Quincy, IL	1920	The chief is provided with a 2-passenger, Buick car, purchased in 1914.
Quincy, IL	1927	The chief is provided with a Buick roadster, purchased in 1925.
Quincy, IL	1941	The chief is provided with a 1939 Ford coupe.
Quincy, MA	1957	A 1953 Ford, 4-door sedan is provided for the chief and two 1955 Chevrolet 4-door sedans are provided for the deputy chiefs and the fire prevention bureau.
Racine, WI	1924	The chief is provided with a Case touring car. It is equipped with gas mask and electric lantern.
Raleigh, NC	1949	Two Dodge sedans, purchased in 1948, are used for the chief and the assistant chief and are equipped with 2 way radios for use with the police radio system.
Revere, MA	1960	Three 4-door sedans, purchased between 1952 and 1957, are provided for the chief, deputy chiefs, and fire prevention officer.
Richmond, CA	1952	The chief drives a 1948 Buick sedan and the assistant and battalion chiefs on duty drive 1951 Mercury station wagons. These latter two vehicles each carry a dry chemical extinguisher, a Scott Air-Pak self-contained breathing apparatus, a stretcher, a portable radio set and a resuscitator with extra oxygen. Four Fords are assigned to the Fire Prevention Bureau, a 1948 Pontiac is used by the drillmaster and a 1948 Buick is used as a spare or reserve car.
Richmond, IN	1940	The chief is provided with a 1933 Dodge coupe, equipped with a radio receiving set.
Richmond, VA	1933	The chief, assistant chief and the two battalion chiefs on duty are each provided with an automobile; one chief's car is in reserve. Motorcycles, with side cars carrying 150 to 250 feet of 1/2-inch rubber hose, 2 portable chemical extinguishers, ax, plaster hook, a pump and bucket, wire brooms, etc., are located with Engine Companies 1, 2, 5, 6, 9, 10, 12, 14 and 15, for use on grass, automobile and chimney fires, and are manned by two men from these companies. Motorcycles, 10 in service. Chief's automobiles, 4 in service, 1 in reserve.
Richmond, VA	1952	There are seven 4-door sedans for the use of the chief, the two battalion chiefs on duty, the chief in charge of the fire prevention bureau, the fire prevention inspectors and the drillmaster. The chief has a 1948 DeSoto; the others are Fords purchased between 1946 and 1951. One 4-door Ford sedan purchased in 1950 is in reserve. All of the cars are 2-way radio equipped and carry one filter type gas mask and one self-contained breathing apparatus, a first-aid kit, electric hand light, hydrant wrench and pair of wire cutters.
Riverside, CA	1958	A 1954 Chevrolet sedan is provided for the chief, a 1953 Chevrolet sedan for the assistant chief, and a 1956 Ford station wagon is used by the battalion chiefs.
Roanoke, VA	1915	The chief is provided with a rubber-tired buggy.
Roanoke, VA	1949	A 1947 Plymouth 4-door sedan is provided for the chief and a 1941 Chevrolet 4-door sedan for the assistant chiefs; both are equipped with three-way radio and some emergency equipment.
Rochester, NY	1922	An automobile is provided for the use of the chief, deputy chief, each battalion chief on duty, the supervisor of engines, and the superintendent of fire alarms. Two chief's cars are in reserve.
Rochester, NY	1950	Twelve sedans are provided for the use of chief officers and maintenance and staff directors. Cars of the chief, deputy chief, deputy chief maintenance division, 4 battalion chiefs and the captain of the arson squad are equipped with two-way radios on police wave length.
Rock Hill, SC		The chief is provided with a 1954, 4-door Chevrolet sedan which is three-way radio equipped.
Rock Island, IL	1932	The chief is provided with a Buick roadster.
Rock Island, IL	1954	The chief is provided with a 1953 Chevrolet 4-door sedan.
Rockford, IL	1909	The marshal owns a 20-horsepower runabout automobile, in which he attends fires. He and the assistant marshal also have horse drawn buggies.
Rockford, IL	1932	The chief is provided with a 1927, 5-passenger sedan, and the assistant chiefs each have a 1930, 5-passenger sedan.
Rome, GA	1907	Chief's wagons, 1 in service.
Rome, GA	1957	The chief is provided with a 1956 Oldsmobile 4-door sedan which carries a small amount of minor equipment.
Rome, NY	1924	The chief is provided with a 7-passenger Reo automobile. The assistant chief responds on the pumper.

Rome, NY	1949	An Oldsmobile sedan purchased in 1947 is provided for the chief officer on duty. The chief uses his personal car at all times when not at headquarters.
Roswell, NM	1952	A 1949 Ford sedan, equipped with two-way radio on the police system is provided for the chief.
Royal Oak, MI	1957	A 1954 Ford sedan and a 1953 Chevrolet coupe are provided for the chief and the assistant chief, respectively, a 1954 Ford sedan for the fire marshal, and a 1954 Chevrolet panel truck for general use.
S. Omaha, NE	1907	Chief's wagons, 1 in service.
Sacramento, CA	1911	The chief is provided with an automobile, which is in poor condition. The assistant chief is provided with a buggy.
Sacramento, CA	1956	Five 1953 and 1955 Buick, Chevrolet and Ford sedans are provided for use by the chief and assistant and battalion chiefs.
Saginaw, MI	1911	Wagons, Chief's, 1 in service.
Saginaw, MI	1922	A Cadillac roadster is provided for the use of the chief. Each of the assistant chiefs has a light Ford truck for use in responding to alarms and also for use as fuel and emergency trucks in case of large fires.
Salem, MA	1916	The chief is provided with a 2-passenger Buick automobile.
Salem, MA	1956	The chief is provided with a 1948 Dodge 4-door sedan and the deputy chief on duty with a 1953 Plymouth 4-door sedan; both are 3-way FM radio equipped.
Salem, OR	1924	The chief owns a touring car in which he drives to such fires as occur while he is away from the station; when at the station, he rides with Hose 1.
Salem, OR	1938	A Model A Ford roadster is furnished the chief.
Salina, KS	1927	Chief's Automobile and Hose Wagon, 1 in service.
Salina, KS	1950	The chief is provided with a 1947 Hudson sedan, equipped with a three-way radio and one oxygen-type mask.
Salt Lake City, UT	1909	Chief's wagons, 2 in service.
Salt Lake City, UT	1954	Chiefs' automobiles include sedans for the chief and fire marshal and coupes for each of the other three assistant chiefs, the four battalion chiefs and the shop superintendent; all are radio equipped. Other automobiles include two coupes and a sedan for the fire prevention bureau, a sedan for the training division, a sedan for the signal division and a spare sedan for the fire force.
San Diego, CA	1910	1 car and 1 buggy in service, 2 buggies in reserve.
San Diego, CA	1957	A 1955 Oldsmobile sedan and a 1954 Ford sedan are assigned to the chief and the assistant chief, respectively. A 1951 Buick sedan and a 1950 Dodge sedan are in reserve. Two 1954 Ford and two 1953 Chevrolet station wagons are assigned to the battalion chiefs on duty and two Ford sedans are in reserve for battalion chiefs. Each of the battalion chief's cars carries a self-contained breathing apparatus, a filter type mask, a resuscitator, smoke ejector, explosimeter, first-aid kit, sprinkler heads and tongs, and a small carbon dioxide extinguisher. The reserve chief's cars are housed at various stations and are occasionally driven by the company members.
San Francisco, CA	1920	Each chief on duty has an automobile; in addition are the following: 8 for hydrant inspection, 3 for repair service, 2 delivery trucks and 6 reserve. Horse-drawn vehicles in service consist of 17 wagons used for supply, wrecking, stables, etc. 5 buggies and 2 carts, with 6 buggies and 6 carts, in good condition, for reserve.
San Francisco, CA	1932	Automobiles are provided for the fire commissioner, chief, each assistant chief and battalion chief on duty, the fire prevention bureau and the department physician. Miscellaneous automobiles and trucks are used in high pressure system maintenance, delivery of supplies, and wrecking and repair service. 22 in service, 5 in reserve.
San Francisco, CA		1948 Sedans are provided for the fire commissioners, chief and assistant chief officers and coupes for battalion chiefs, members of the fire prevention bureau, mechanics, instructors and the salvage captain. Various trucks and automobiles are used in high pressure system maintenance, delivery of supplies and in repair service. 34 Chief cars in service, 17 in reserve.
San Jose, CA	1932	A Nash roadster of 1928 model is provided for use of the hazard inspector. The chief drives his own car to fires and allowance is made by the city for use of private cars of the fire marshal and hydrant inspector.
Sandusky, OH	1922	The chief is provided with a Ford roadster.
Santa Ana, CA	1937	Light sedans of 1932 and 1934 models are furnished for the chief and fire marshal.
Santa Barbara, CA	1927	A Dodge roadster of 1925 model with chemical extinguisher, ax, shovel, and garden hose is provided for the chief and a like car of 1922 model for the inspector. A light delivery car in poor condition is used to carry supplies and wet hose.
Santa Barbara, CA	1937	Dodge or Ford sedans of 1930 model are furnished the chief officers. Three other cars, 2 of which are in poor condition, are used by the mechanic, the fire marshal, and for carrying wet hose.
Santa Barbara, CA	1946	Pontiac and Chevrolet sedans, both equipped with 2-way radio, are furnished for the chief and deputy chief on duty. The fire marshal uses a Chevrolet pickup truck, equipped with 100-gallon tank, booster pump and two-way radio, during the dry grass season; at other times he drives a Ford sedan which has two-way radio equipment.
Santa Barbara, CA	1953	Additional department vehicles include the chief's 1950 Ford sedan, the assistant chief's 1951 Ford sedan, the fire marshal's 1946 Ford sedan, the inspector's 1948 Chevrolet pickup truck with booster tank and pump, the master mechanic's 1950 Chevrolet panel truck and a 1938 Chevrolet pickup truck. All are equipped with 3-way radio, except the 1938 pickup truck, which has a receiver only.
Savannah, GA	1905	Chief's wagons, 2 in service.
Savannah, GA	1950	A 1948 Cadillac sedan is provided for the chief and two 1950 Oldsmobile sedans are used by the battalion chiefs on duty; a 1943 Buick sedan is in reserve. A 1939 Lincoln sedan, carrying a resuscitator, is used for emergency calls. All automobiles are equipped with 3-way radio.

Schenectady, NY	1920	The chief and deputy chief are each provided with a 4-passenger automobile. The deputy fire marshal has a motorcycle with side car. Auxiliary squad is equipped with a 7-passenger touring car carrying 200 feet of garden hose, 4 extinguishers, rope, 5 gas masks, flash lights and lanterns.
Schenectady, NY	1953	There are three sedans provided for the chief officers. The chief has a 1948 Cadillac, the responding deputy a 1952 Packard and the assistant chief and deputy in charge of training share a 1950 Hudson. All three of these cars are equipped with three-way FM radio and carry a few small appliances. A 1951 Chevrolet with a suburban body is available as a general utility car.
Seattle, WA	1906	Chief's wagons, 4 in service; in reserve, none; all in good condition. The four officers wagons include one cart used by the hydrant inspector.
Seattle, WA	1910	The chief and the first assistant chief are each provided with a 4-cylinder gasoline motor car and a horse and buggy, only one other assistant chief is provided with a rig.
Seattle, WA	1954	In addition to the six first-aid cars, the department has 15 Chevrolet sedans with ages varying between 2 and 14 years, including one for the chief, one for the assistant chief, one for each of the 5 battalion chiefs on duty.
Sedalia, MO	1945	The chief and assistant chief respond on apparatus when on duty, and the chief responds in his private car when off duty; no allowance is made for such use.
Selma, AL	1957	A 1954 Dodge sedan is provided for the use of the chief and the assistant chief. It carries a pair of rubber gloves and wire cutters.
Shaker Heights, OH	1948	The chief is provided with a 1947 Buick sedan, equipped with three-way radio.
Shawnee, OK	1931	A Hupmobile, 1924 model roadster, is provided for the chief. This car is in poor condition and not well adapted for the service.
Sheboygan, WI	1954	A 1953 Chevrolet sedan is provided for the use of the chief; it carries only a small chemical extinguisher. A 1952 Chevrolet sedan is provided for the use of the assistant chiefs; it carries two self-contained breathing apparatus and some other minor equipment.
Shreveport, LA	1911	The chief has an automobile, which carries a portable extinguisher and an ax. It was built in 1907 and is in poor condition. The Chief's buggy is held in reserve; it is used ordinarily for fire alarm work. The assistant chief attends fires with Hose Company No. 3.
Shreveport, LA	1924	The chief has a 1923 model Cadillac and the assistant chief a 1922 Buick runabout, both of which are in good condition.
Sioux City, IA	1913	Buggies are provided for the chief and assistant chief.
Sioux City, IA	1947	Two sedans with a third in reserve, are provided for use of chief officers; the two in service have two-way radios and the assistant chief's car is equipped with a carbon-dioxide extinguisher, fog nozzle and two self-contained breathing apparatus.
Sioux Falls, SD	1924	A Packard 1923 roadster is provided for the chief. It is also used as a supply car when needed. A Maxwell 1923 touring car is used for a supply car and for general department business.
Sioux Falls, SD	1951	A 1948 sedan is provided for the chief. A 1948 Chevrolet sedan delivery truck, carrying emergency and rescue equipment, is used by the assistant chiefs in responding to fires.
Somerville, MA	1958	The chief is provided with a 1951 Cadillac 4-door sedan, and three 1953 Ford sedans are provided for use by the deputy and district chiefs. A radio is in each chief officer automobile.
South Bend, IN	1911	Chief's wagons, 3 in service.
South Bend, IN	1920	The chief is provided with a 2-passenger Studebaker automobile, which carries stilson wrenches, a bolt cutter, gas mask, electric hand lantern and large blanket. There is a buggy in reserve.
South Bend, IN	1942	Two automobiles, both with two-way radio equipment, are provided for chief officers and another for the inspector; all are of Studebaker make. A 21-year-old White hose wagon is used for supply service.
South Gate, CA	1949	A Ford sedan is provided for chief officers, and a Chevrolet sedan is assigned to the fire prevention bureau; both are equipped with 2-way radio. The chief used his private car which is not equipped as an emergency vehicle.
Spartanburg, SC	1958	A 1951 Oldsmobile sedan, equipped with a fair supply of minor equipment, is provided for the use of the chief officers.
Spokane, WA	1910	The chief engineer is provided with a 4-cylinder gasoline motor car and the assistant chief with a horse and buggy.
Spokane, WA	1927	A roadster is provided for the chief, a touring car for each assistant chief. Chiefs' cars carry gas mask, hydrant wrench, sprinkler head tongs, rubber gloves and a portable extinguishers. A chief's automobile is in reserve.
Springfield, IL	1908	Chief's wagons, 2 in service.
Springfield, IL	1921	The chief is provided with a 5-passenger National automobile; a second car has been taken out of service recently so that at present there is no car for the assistant chiefs.
Springfield, IL	1949	Two cars are provided for use of the chief and the district chief. The chief's car is equipped with a mobile telephone unit and with some minor equipment; district chief's car carries an inhalator, one self-contained mask, rubber gloves, and minor tools.
Springfield, MO	1918	The chief is provided with a 1916 Jeffery roadster; the assistant chief rides on the automobile chemical engine, which is of double tank type, with airless tires, dual on rear wheels.
Springfield, MO	1928	The chief is provided with a 2-passenger Studebaker automobile.
Springfield, OH	1921	There is a four passenger automobile, in fair condition purchased second hand in 1919, for the use of the chief.
Springfield, OH	1955	The chief, the assistant chief, the drillmaster, and the chief of the fire prevention bureau are provided with late model sedans. A 1954 Ford station wagon, equipped with some appliances and first aid equipment, is used by the platoon chiefs.

Springfield, OH	1960	3 chiefs' cars in service.
St. Cloud, MN	1950	The chief is provided with a 1938 coupe.
St. Joseph, MO	1907	Chief's wagons, 2 in service, 1 in reserve.
St. Joseph, MO	1947	Each of the chief officers is provided with a 1937 or 1938 Oldsmobile or a Pontiac sedan, equipped with two-way radio; a 1932 Ford coupe is in reserve.
St. Louis, MO	1920	The chief is provided with a seven-passenger automobile, and each assistant chief with a two-passenger roadster. There are no reserve chiefs' machines, but several chiefs' buggies are kept for use in emergency.
St. Louis, MO	1950	The chief is provided with a 1948 Chrysler sedan. 11 cars in service, 2 cars in reserve.
St. Paul, MN	1907	Wagons, Chief's and Fire Alarm Supt. 6 in service, 2 in reserve
St. Paul, MN	1931	The chief is provided with a Packard sedan. A Buick coupe and 4 roadsters are used by the assistant and district chiefs. Cars are provided for the use of the superintendent of apparatus and chief inspector of the fire prevention bureau. A spare chief's car is kept at headquarters.
St. Paul, MN	1951	The chief is provided with a 1948 Packard sedan, and all other chief officers on duty, the chief of the Fire Prevention Bureau, and the superintendent of apparatus are provided with 1947 Ford coaches; one reserve chief's car is available.
St. Petersburg, FL	1926	A Hudson touring car is provided for the chief.
St. Petersburg, FL	1939	A Ford coupe is provided for the chief. The assistant chief rides with the chief or on the apparatus or in his own car.
St. Petersburg, FL	1963	The fire department operates its own radio system and all vehicles in the department are equipped with transmitter-receivers. A portable unit is carried in each of the district chief's cars. 4 chief's cars in service.
Stamford, CT	1952	A 1950 4-door Dodge sedan and a 1949 4-door Nash sedan are provided for the chief and deputy chief, respectively. Both vehicles are 3-way radio equipped and carry a variety of minor tools. A 1949 4-door Plymouth sedan is assigned to the fire prevention inspector.
Stockton, CA	1905	Chief wagon, 1 in service.
Stockton, CA	1929	Cadillac, Peerless and Essex touring cars are furnished for the chief, assistant chief and master mechanic. The chief's car carries extinguishers, shut-off nozzle, fittings, adapters and a punch register.
Stockton, CA	1935	A Studebaker sedan is provided for the chief and a Buick sedan for the first assistant chief. Each car is equipped with radio receiver, telephone, gas mask, ax, portable extinguishers and hydrant wrenches. A Studebaker sedan is provided for the master mechanic.
Stockton, CA	1952	Three radio-equipped sedans are provided for chief officers; the chief has a 1947 Oldsmobile, the first assistant chiefs a 1951 DeSoto and the second assistant chiefs a 1948 Chevrolet. A 1949 Chevrolet is used by the Fire Prevention Bureau.
Stratford, CT	1950	A 1947 Chevrolet sedan is provided for the assistant chief and is two-way radio equipped. The chief generally uses his own private car or rides with the assistant chief.
Stubenville, OH	1928	The chief is provided with a Studebaker roadster.
Stubenville, OH	1946	The chief is provided with a 1940 Buick sedan which carries a small amount of minor equipment.
Superior, WI	1908	Chief's wagons, 2 in service, 1 in reserve.
Superior, WI	1914	The city provides a 60 horse-power, 5-passenger Oakland car for the chief, a motorcycle for the master mechanic and a bicycle at each station for the use of firemen detailed on inspection work. There is a chief's buggy in reserve. The assistant chief goes on the squad wagon.
Superior, WI	1930	The chief is provided with a Chrysler touring car, and a Lincoln 7-passenger touring car is used by the assistant chiefs and a squad car.
Syracuse, NY	1917	Five chief automobiles in service (2 chief automobiles in service in 1914). Two wagons is reserve.
Syracuse, NY	1950	Twelve automobiles are provided for the use of chief officers, shop crew, instructor, fire marshal and the superintendent of fire alarms. All chief officers' cars are equipped with two way radios.
Tacoma, WA	1905	Chief's wagons, 2 in service, 2 in reserve.
Tacoma, WA	1928	A Buick roadster is provided for the chief and another for the assistant chief on duty.
Tallahassee, FL	1955	The chief is provided with a 1954 Hudson 4-door sedan and a 1953 Chevrolet 4-door sedan is provided for the assistant chief on duty, both being equipped with 3-way radio on the police system.
Tampa, FL	1907	Chief's wagons; 2 in service, 0 in reserve.
Tampa, FL	1952	The Chief is provided with a 1951 Oldsmobile 4-door sedan and the assistant chief on duty with a 1951 Chevrolet 4-door sedan; both are 3-way radio equipped. The fire marshal is provided a 1948 Chevrolet 4-door sedan, and there are two 1946 Chevrolet 4-door sedans used by the inspectors of the fire prevention bureau.
Texarkana, AR	1923	The chief is provided with a Buick roadster and carries first-aid kit, searchlight and oxygen helmet. The assistant chief is provided with a Stutz roadster and carries no fire-fighting equipment.
Texarkana, AR	1935	The chief is provided with a Lincoln touring car which carries no fire fighting facilities.
Texarkana, AR	1950	The Arkansas and the Texas chiefs are equipped with 1949 and 1942 sedans, respectively, the former equipped with 2-way radio and the latter with radio receiver only. Neither department has any pickup truck for fire alarm or other departmental work, being dependent on the chief's cars.
Toledo, OH	1917	The chief, assistant and each district chief is provided with a 2-passenger automobile and a 5-passenger touring car is in reserve. 6 in service, 1 in reserve.
Toledo, OH	1959	The chief is provided with a 1956 sedan, and the deputy chief and the district chiefs on duty with 1953, 1957 or 1958 sedans. One chief's car is in reserve. 13 in service, 1 in reserve.
Topeka, KS	1928	The chief is provided with a high-speed roadster carrying an oxygen helmet, 3-gallon extinguisher, surgical kit and electric lantern. The assistant chief is provided with a similar car and equipped with a gas mask and lung motor.

Topeka, KS	1954	The chief and the platoon assistant chief on duty are provided with new Ford Ranch Wagons carrying some special equipment. The first assistant chief and the deputy inspector are provided with 1949 Pontiac coupes.
Torrington, CT	1958	The chief is provided with a 1955 Plymouth 2-door sedan; the deputy chief has no automobile and rides one of the pumpers.
Trenton, NJ	1914	The chief is provided with a 5-passenger 20-horsepower Stanley steam automobile and the assistant chiefs with a 25-horsepower Haynes automobile carrying a 30-gallon Holloway chemical tank, 300 feet of chemical hose and two 2-1/2-gallon extinguishers.
Trenton, NJ	1954	There are three sedans provided for chief officers. The chief and each of the two deputy chiefs on duty are provided with an Oldsmobile sedan purchased in 1948, 1949 and 1950, respectively. These cars are equipped with a few small appliances; a 1941 Buick sedan is in reserve. All chief's cars are equipped with one-way FM radio, operating on the police department frequency.
Tuscaloosa, AL	1938	The chief is provided with an automobile; the assistant chief's automobile was badly damaged in a recent accident and may not be replaced.
Tuscaloosa, AL	1957	The chief is provided with a 1956 Oldsmobile and the assistant chiefs with a 1955 Ford; both are 4-door sedans and radio equipped. Use of the assistant chief's car is shared with the Fire Prevention Bureau.
Union City, NJ	1956	There are three chief officers' cars in service, all being 1953 or 1954 Plymouth 4-door sedans. All are three-way radio equipped on the police department system and each carries a first-aid kit, a hand light and a small carbon dioxide hand extinguisher. A 1946 Buick 4-door sedan, also radio equipped and provided with an amplifying system with 2 speakers mounted on the roof, is provided for the use of the fire prevention inspector.
University City, MO	1929	The chief is provided with a Studebaker closed car purchased in 1928.
University City, MO	1946	The chief is provided with a 1937 Chevrolet coupe, but normally rides on the hose-ladder truck when responding to alarms.
Valdosta, GA	1957	The chief is provided a 1953 Ford, 4-door sedan which carries no minor equipment. The assistant chief is not provided a car but rides on the first piece of apparatus leaving headquarters when he is responding to alarms.
Vancouver, WA	1956	A 1952 Pontiac sedan is used by the chief; a 1954 Ford sedan by the assistant chief and a 1955 Chevrolet sedan by the battalion chief on duty.
Vernon, CA	1941	The chief uses his personal car to answer alarms from his residence in Huntington Park.
W. New York, NJ	1917	The chief is provided with a Ford automobile, carrying 2 chemical extinguishers and a surgical kit.
W. New York, NJ	1959	1952 Pontiac and 1953 Ford sedans, radio-equipped on the police radio system, are provided for the use of the chief officers and the inspectors.
W. Palm Beach, FL	1935	A Studebaker sedan is provided for the chief and a Buick touring car for the assistant chief.
W. Palm Beach, FL	1952	The chief is provided with a 1949 Packard sedan and the assistant chiefs with a 1949 Pontiac 2-door sedan.
Walla Walla, WA	1949	A 1942 sedan, equipped with three-way radio, is provided for the chief and two coupes for the assistant chief.
Waltham, MA	1915	The chief's car is a 45-horsepower, 4-passenger, Rambler automobile, equipped with a 25-gallon chemical tank and 150 feet of chemical hose. A rubber-tired buggy with swinging harness is in reserve.
Warren, MI	1960	The commissioner and the chief are provided with 1958 and 1957 sedans, respectively, and the assistant chief, master mechanic and fire inspector have 1958 or 1959 station wagons.
Warren, OH	1958	A 1953 Oldsmobile sedan and a 4-door Buick station wagon are provided for the use of the chief and his assistants.
Waterbury, CT	1941	A 1937 Packard sedan, equipped with a two-way radio and carrying a small amount of minor equipment, including a tannic acid kit is provided the chief. A 1933 Buick sedan, equipped with a one-way radio and carrying some minor equipment, including a sprinkler kit, tannic acid kit and 2 gas masks, is provided the deputy chief. A 1934 Nash sedan is provided the fire marshal, and a 1929 Cadillac sedan is held in reserve.
Watertown, MA	1937	The chief is provided with a Packard coupe.
Watertown, NY	1915	The chief is provided with an automobile and a rubber tired buggy in reserve.
Watertown, NY	1953	A 1952 Pontiac 4-door sedan and a 1950 Pontiac 2-door coupe are provided for the chief and the deputy chiefs, respectively. Both vehicles are radio equipped on the police department frequency with only a receiver in the chief's car but a receiver and transmitter in the other car.
Waukegan, IL	1940	The chief is provided with a 1934 Ford coupe, and a 1925 Cadillac car has been fitted for line use.
Waukegan, IL	1955	The chief's car and the two rescue trucks are 1952 Ford station wagons; the rescue trucks carry some emergency equipment.
Wausau, WI	1953	A 1950 Mercury sedan is provided for the use of the chief; it is equipped with considerable fire-fighting, salvage and first-aid appliances.
Wauwatosa, WI	1953	The chief is provided with a 1952 Ford 4-door sedan, equipped with a two-way radio. The assistant chief uses either the chief's car or responds to fires with an engine company. A 1949 Willys jeep is used by the fire inspector.
Weirton, WV	1950	The chief uses his own automobile for fire department purposes and receives an allowance to defray expenses involved.
West Allis, WI	1932	The chief is provided with a 1928 Hudson sedan.
West Allis, WI	1956	A 1948 Pontiac and a 1954 Ford, both 4-door sedans, are provided for the chief and assistant chief's, respectively.
Wheeling, WV	1913	The chief is provided with an automobile and the first assistant chief with a rubber-tired buggy.

Wheeling, WV	1950	The chief uses his own automobile, a 1947 Chrysler 5-passenger coupe equipped with 2-way radio, and is reimbursed by the city. A 1949 Ford coupe is furnished for the assistant chief.
White Plains, NY	1957	A 1954 Pontiac and a 1955 Plymouth are provided for the use of the chief and deputy chiefs, respectively. Two additional automobiles are provided for use by the fire prevention inspector, the master mechanic, and other department personnel. All carry a small amount of minor equipment.
Whittier, CA	1957	A 1955 Mercury sedan is assigned to the chief and a 1954 Ford station wagon is assigned to the assistant chief on duty. A 1952 Pontiac sedan and a 1950 Pontiac business coupe are assigned to the Fire Prevention Bureau for use by the captain in charge of the bureau and by the shift inspectors.
Wilkes Barre, PA	1917	The chief is provided with a Stutz car purchased in 1916. It carries a lung motor, lock breaker, ax, hose shut-off, revolving nozzle, Helm nozzle, revolving nozzle tip, rivet cutter, tin roof cutter, electric searchlight, rip saw, two 3-gallon extinguishers, 150 feet of 1/2-inch rope, life belt, rubber gloves, 2 smoke protectors and 1 hand search-light.
Wilkes Barre, PA	1929	The chief is provided with a Studebaker touring car purchased in 1924.
Wilkes Barre, PA	1953	The chief is provided with a 1946 Buick 4-door sedan. The car formerly provided the assistant chief on duty has been reassigned to the city building inspector. The assistant chief must share the car with the chief during the day but usually has sole use of it at night. This car is 3-way FM radio equipped on the police department frequency, and is provided with a small amount of minor equipment which includes two filter-type gas masks, a first-aid kit, a carbon dioxide extinguisher, handlight, a double male and female connection.
Wilkinsburg, PA	1958	A 1957 Chrysler sedan is provided for the use of the chief and deputy chiefs.
Williamsport, PA	1914	The city furnishes a horse and buggy for the chief. This is kept at Station 4, although the chief's headquarters is at Station 2.
Williamsport, PA	1960	A 1958 station wagon and a 1954 sedan are provided for the chief and fire prevention inspector, respectively.
Wilmington, DE	1914	The city provides an automobile runabout for the chief, and a horse and buggy for each assistant chief. A spare buggy and harness is in reserve.
Wilmington, DE	1950	There are 6 chief officers' cars in service. The chief is provided with a 1946 Lincoln 4-door sedan and each deputy chief, each assistant chief and the fire marshal have 1947 Ford 2-door sedan. All except the fire marshal's car are equipped with 2-way FM radio and carry some minor equipment.
Wilmington, NC	1921	The chief is provided with a light roadster and a driver from each platoon.
Wilmington, NC	1958	1956 Oldsmobile and 1953 Chevrolet sedans are provided for the use of the chief and the assistant chief, respectively. Both are three-way radio equipped.
Winona, MN	1952	The chief is provided with a 1942 Dodge sedan.
Winston Salem, NC	1949	A 1941 and 1937 Buick sedan are provided for the chief and the assistant chief, respectively. Both cars carry a large variety of minor equipment and are equipped with two-way radios.
Winston Salem, NC	1956	The chief is provided with a 1951 Buick sedan, the assistant chief a 1955 Dodge station wagon, and the supervisor of training a 1955 Ford sedan.
Woonsocket, RI	1911	Chief's wagons, 2 in service, owned by chief and assistant.
Woonsocket, RI	1954	A 1947 Dodge sedan is provided for the chief and a 1947 Plymouth sedan for the deputy or assistant or battalion chief.
Worcester, MA	1952	The chief and each deputy and district chief on duty are provided with a 4-door sedan. The chief has a 1949 Buick, the deputy chief a 1949 Dodge and the district chiefs a 1949 and 1951 Dodge; all of these cars are two-way radio equipped. In addition, there are two 1943 Buick sedans and 1943 Dodge coupe provided for the Fire Prevention Bureau, a 1947 Ford coupe for the district chief in charge of fire alarm. A 1941 Buick sedan is in reserve; of these cars only the reserve chief's car is radio equipped. The cars used by the chief officers of the fire force are all uniformly equipped, each carrying an aspirating nozzle for liquid foam, a first-aid kit, a hydrant wrench, a spray nozzle for use on 2-1/2-inch hose, 3 filter-type gas masks, and a self-contained breathing apparatus; in addition, the deputy chief's car carries a spray-type cellar pipe.
Worchester, MA	1913	The chief, deputy chief, and two district chiefs are provided with automobiles; those for the last three were placed in service November, 1912; four rubber-tired buggies are in reserve. The superintendent of fire alarm telegraph has a rubber-tired buggy.
Wyandotte, MI	1952	A 1950 Ford sedan, equipped with a three-way radio on the police frequency, is provided for the use of the chief officers.
Yakima, WA	1933	A Studebaker coupe is furnished for use of the chief and a Chevrolet roadster for the assistant chief.
Yakima, WA	1951	A 1951 Chevrolet sedan serves as chief's car and a 1949 Chevrolet sedan as assistant chief's car.
Yonkers, NY	1911	The chief and assistant chiefs are provided with horse drawn buggies; one is in reserve. Automobiles for the chiefs have been authorized.
Yonkers, NY	1957	The chief is provided with a 1954 Packard 4-door sedan and the eastern and western assistant chiefs are provided with a 1955 Ford 2-door sedan and a 1953 Packard 4-door sedan, respectively; all have three-way radio equipment and carry a small amount of emergency and minor equipment. The department has 6 assistant chiefs.
Youngstown, OH	1912	The chief is provided with a 5-passenger automobile. The assistant chiefs respond to alarms of fire on the automobile combination hose wagon.
Zanesville, OH	1927	The chief is provided with a Buick roadster, purchased in 1925. Equipment includes a foam-type extinguisher and a siren. A former car of the chief is now used for fire alarm maintenance and general utility.

PHOTO CREDITS

A

AACA Library &
    Research Center
Don P. Abrahamson
Richard Adelman
Glen Alton

B

Glenn Banz
Bare Cove Museum
Dick Bartlett
Roger J. Birchfield
Roger Bjorge
Charles Black
Ron Bogardus
Mark Boock
Box 388 Productions
Herb Brawley
H.L. Brenner
W. Parker Browne

C

John A. Calderone
John M. Calderone
T.J. Carpenter
William Cary
Edward Christopher
Steve Cloutier
Marvin Cohen
Gene Conway
James T. Coyne

D

James Derstine
Leo Duliba

E

Ed Effron
Bill Egan
Tim Elder
Bill Elliott
Thomas Engle

F

Charles H. Fewster
John D. Floyd, Jr.
Paul G. Fox
Edward G. Frey
Fred Fuston

G

W.G. Garrison
Jackson Gerhart
Greater Harrisburg
    Fire Museum

H

Ed Haas
Eric Hansen
Ralph Harkins
B.A. Harper
Ron Helman
Shelton Hensley Family
Tommy Herman
Michael Hink
David Houseal

J

Don Jarvis
Daniel Jasina
Ronald Jeffers
R.D. Jennings

K

Wayne Kidd
William Killen
Hank Knight
Arthur Knobloch
Karl Krouch
Robert Kulp

L

Matt Lee
Ken Little
Steve Loftin

M

Dale Magee
The Mand Library &
    Research Center
Dan Martin
Keith Marvin
Alex Matches
Walt McCall
Aston N. McKenney
Bob Muller

N

Louis E. Nelson
Bill Noonan
Gordon J. Nord, Jr.

P

Jack Paxton
Edward L. Peterson
Kenneth E. Peterson
William Phillips
Robert Potter

R

Racine Firebell Museum
    Association
Jack Ramsey
J.F. Repp
Charles W. Reynolds
John J. Robrecht
Ernest Rodriques
Paul Romano
Harry Rosenblum
Michael Rybarczyk

S

Hank Sajovic
Len Sasher
John J. Schaler III
Bob Schierle
John Schimdt
Scott Schimpf
David Schnell
Walt Schryver
William N. Schwartz
Charles A. Seaboyer
Bill Snyder
Wayne Sorensen
Craig Stewart
Richard L. Story
Wayne Stuart

T

Frank Tremel
Toledo Firefighters Museum

W

Robert Washburn
Deran Watt
William T. Wilcox
Bob Willever
William Witt
Randy Wootton

Y

York Fire Museum

MANUFACTURER INDEX